You Can Cook Better:

My Cooking Recipe Book

Wanda J. Moore

PEACH SHORTCAKE

Yolk of one egg,
One-half cup of sugar.

Cream well and then add

Three tablespoons of shortening,
Four tablespoons of water,
One cup of flour,
Two teaspoonfuls of baking powder,
One-half teaspoon of vanilla.

Beat to thoroughly mix and then bake in well-greased deep layer-cake pan in a moderate oven for twenty minutes. Cook and then split and fill with well-drained canned crushed peaches. Place together. Now place white of egg and one-half glass of apple jelly in a bowl; beat with Dover egg-beater until the mixture forms into a stiff meringue.

BANANA SHORTCAKE

One-half cup of sugar,
Four tablespoons of shortening,
One egg.

Place in a mixing bowl and then cream well, then add

One and one-quarter cups of sifted flour,
Three level teaspoons of baking powder,
One level teaspoon of vanilla extract,
One-half cup of water.

Beat to mix and pour into well-greased and floured oblong baking pans. Now spread the top of the cake with three bananas sliced very thin. Place in a moderate oven and bake for thirty-five minutes. Use the white of egg and half glass of apple jelly for a meringue.

OLDVIRGINIASHOR TCAKE

Sift the flour and then fill a quart measure, using a tablespoon to lift the flour. Care should be taken not to shake or pack the flour down, as the quart of flour should weigh just one pound. Place in a bowl and add

Three level tablespoons of baking powder,
One teaspoon of salt,
Three-quarters cup of sugar.

Sift again to mix and then rub in one-half cup of shortening. Place one and one-half cups of buttermilk in a pitcher and add one teaspoon of baking soda. Stir to thoroughly dissolve the soda and then use this to mix the flour to a dough. Knead well in the bowl with a spoon and then turn on a slightly floured board and roll or pat out one inch thick. Cut with a large biscuit cutter and brush the top with shortening and bake in a hot oven for eighteen minutes.

APRICOTSHOR TCAKE

One-half cup of sugar,
Four tablespoons of shortening,
Yolk of one egg.

Cream until light and frothy, and then add

Four tablespoons of water,
One cup of flour,
Two level teaspoons of baking powder.

Beat to thoroughly mix and then pour into well-greased layer cake pan. Bake for twenty minutes in a moderate oven. Split and fill with cooked apricots and then place in a bowl

White of one egg, left over,
One-half glass of jelly.

Beat to thoroughly mix with the Dover egg-beater until it forms a stiff meringue. Pile on top of cake and garnish with single piece of apricot.

HUCKLEBERRY SHORTCAKE

Place in a mixing bowl

Three-quarters cup of sugar,
One egg,
Four tablespoons of shortening,
Two cups of flour,
Four teaspoons of baking powder,
Three-quarters cup of water.

Beat and mix and then pour into well-greased oblong pan and bake in a moderate oven twenty minutes. Cool and then split, and fill with the prepared berries and serve with custard sauce.

To prepare the huckleberries for the shortcake, place in a saucepan

Two cups of stewed huckleberries,
One-half cup of cornstarch,
One cup of brown sugar.

Stir to dissolve and then bring to a boil and cook slowly for five minutes. Add one-half teaspoon of nutmeg and then cool and use for the filling.

LEMON DUMPLINGS

Place in a bowl:

One tablespoon of baking powder,
One cup of flour,
One and one-half cups of fine bread crumbs,

One cup of chopped suet,
One cup of brown sugar,
Juice of one lemon,
Two eggs,
Grated rind of one-half lemon,
One and one-half cups of milk.

Beat to thoroughly mix and then pour into well-greased mould and boil for one and one-quarter hours. Serve with lemon sauce.

PEACH CAKE

Place in a mixing bowl

Three-quarters cup of sugar,
One egg,
Four tablespoons of shortening,
Two cups of flour,
Four level tablespoons of baking powder,
Three-quarters cup of water.

Beat just enough to mix and then pour into a deep well-greased and floured layer-cake pan. Cover the top thickly with diced peaches and then place in a small bowl

Six tablespoons of flour,
Four tablespoons of sugar,
Two tablespoons of shortening,
One teaspoon of cinnamon.

Rub between the tips of the fingers until crumbly and then spread on the top of the peaches and bake in a moderate oven for thirty minutes.

PEACH DUMPLINGS

Place in a mixing bowl

Two cups of flour,

One teaspoon of salt,
One teaspoon baking powder,
One tablespoon sugar.

Sift to mix and then rub in one-half cup of shortening; then mix to a dough with one-fourth cup of ice-cold water. Set on ice for one hour, then roll out one-eighth inch thick and cut into four-inch squares. Fill with pared and stoned peaches, placing two tablespoons of brown sugar and one-half teaspoon of nutmeg in each dumpling. Brush the edges with water and then fold the pastry together. Place on a well-greased baking sheet and add one-half cup of water to the pan and bake in a moderate oven for thirty minutes.

APPLE CAKE

Place in a bowl

Two cups of flour,

and then add

One-half teaspoon of salt,
Three teaspoons of baking powder,
One and one-half teaspoons of nutmeg.

Sift twice to blend and then rub in five tablespoons of shortening. Break an egg into a cup and then fill cup to the two-thirds mark with milk, beat to blend the egg and milk and then mix into the dough. Roll out one-half inch thick and then line an oblong baking sheet. Pare and cut the apples into quarters and then into thin slices. Place one cup of sugar and one-half cup of water in a saucepan and add the apples, a few at a time, and cook for a few minutes. Lift and lay on the prepared dough. Place in a moderate oven to bake for thirty-five minutes. After the cake is in the oven for eighteen minutes baste frequently with syrup in which the apples were cooked. Ten minutes before removing from the oven sprinkle thickly with brown sugar and cinnamon.

DUMPLINGS FOR STEW

Place in a mixing bowl

One and one-half cups of flour,

and then add

One teaspoon of salt,
Two teaspoons of baking powder,
One-half teaspoon of pepper,
One teaspoon of grated onion.

Add two-thirds cup of water and mix to a dough. Drop by the spoonful into the stew and cover closely and boil for twelve minutes. If you open the lid of the saucepan while the dumplings are cooking they will be heavy.

CHERRY DUMPLINGS

Wash individual pudding cloths in warm water and then rub with shortening and dust slightly with flour. Now place in a bowl

One cup of sugar,
One and one-half cups of flour,
One-half teaspoon of salt,
Three level teaspoons of baking powder,
One-half cup of fine bread crumbs,
One egg,
One cup of milk,
Two cups of stoned cherries.

Mix and then place one cooking spoon of the mixture into each prepared dumpling cloth. Tie loosely and then plunge into boiling water and cook for twenty minutes. Lift into the colander and let drain for three minutes and then serve with stewed cherries for sauce.

STEAMED ROLY POLY PUDDING

One and one-half cups of flour,
One-half teaspoon of salt,

Three teaspoons of baking powder,
Four tablespoons of sugar.

Place in a mixing bowl and sift to mix. Now rub in four tablespoons of shortening and mix to a dough with a scant two-thirds cup of water. Roll out one-half inch thick and spread with well-cleaned huckleberries and then cover quickly with brown sugar. Roll like for jelly roll and then tie in a cloth and plunge into boiling water or place in a steamer and cook for one hour. Serve with fruit sauce.

If using canned huckleberries, drain them well, then thicken the juice and use for sauce. Any variety of fresh fruit may be used.

FRUIT CUP CUSTARDS

Place six nice berries in each custard cup and then place in a mixing bowl

Two cups of milk,
Six tablespoons of sugar,
One-half teaspoon of nutmeg,
Three eggs.

Beat thoroughly to mix and then pour over the berries in the cups. Place in a baking pan containing warm water and bake in a slow oven until firm in the centre.

CREAM TAPIOCA PUDDING

Wash two-thirds cup of tapioca in four or five waters and then place in a saucepan and add one and one-half cups of water. Cook until the tapioca begins to soften, then add one and one-half cups of milk. Cook until soft and then add

One well-beaten egg,
One-half cup of sugar,
One-half teaspoon nutmeg.

Mix well and cook for a few minutes longer. Remove from the fire and serve ice cold with fruit whip.

MACARONI NEAPOLITAN

Cook one-half package of macaroni in boiling water for fifteen minutes and then turn into a colander and place under cold running water. Now mince

One onion and one tomato

fine and place four tablespoons of fat in a frying pan. When hot, add the onion and tomato, cook until soft and then add the macaroni. Toss gently until hot and then cover it closely to prevent drying out. If too dry, add a couple of tablespoons of boiling water. Season with pepper, salt and one-half cup catsup.

MACARONI CUTLETS

Cook one-quarter pound of macaroni in boiling water for twenty minutes and then drain. Cool and then chop fine. Place in a bowl and add

One-half cup of grated cheese,
Two tablespoons of grated onion,
One tablespoon of finely minced parsley,
Two teaspoons of salt,
One teaspoon of paprika,
One-well-beaten egg.

Mix thoroughly and then mould into croquettes. Roll in flour and then dip in beaten egg. Roll in fine crumbs and fry in hot fat. Place in a hot oven for ten minutes to finish cooking.

POLENTA A LA NAPLES

Place in a saucepan

Two and one-half cups of boiling water,
One and one-half teaspoons of salt.

Now pour in very slowly

Three-quarters cup of yellow cornmeal.

Stir to prevent lumping and cook until very thick. Add

Three-quarters cup of cheese, cut into fine pieces,
One onion, chopped fine,
One green pepper, chopped fine,
One leek, chopped fine,
One teaspoon of paprika.

Mix thoroughly and then pour into a large bowl to cool. Form into sausages and then roll in flour and brown in hot oil. Serve with tomato sauce. Wheat cereal may be used to replace the cornmeal.

NOODLES

FRIED NOODLES

Cook noodles in boiling water and then drain. Now mince fine

Three onions,
Two red peppers,
Two leeks.

Place four tablespoons of cooking oil in a frying pan and when hot add the vegetables. Cook slowly until soft and then add the noodles. Toss constantly until a light brown and then pile in the centre of a large platter. Lay a goulash around for a border. Pour the gravy over all and then garnish with two tablespoons of grated cheese and serve.

BOILED HOMINY—CHEESE SAUCE

Soak large hominy over night and then in the morning wash and cook in plenty of boiling water until tender. Drain well and place in a baking dish and cover with cheese sauce, made as follows:

Place one and one-half cups of milk in a saucepan and add two tablespoons of grated onion and four level tablespoons of cornstarch. Dissolve the starch in the milk and bring to a boil. Cook slowly for five minutes and then add

Two tablespoons of chopped parsley,
Two teaspoons of salt,
Two ounces of cheese,
One teaspoon of Worcestershire sauce,
One teaspoon of paprika.

Mix thoroughly and then heat until the cheese melts. Serve as vegetable.

MACARONI AND CHEESE

Cook one package of macaroni in a large kettle of boiling water for twenty minutes and then drain and pour over the macaroni a pan of cold water. Drain again. Now return to the kettle and add

One-half can of tomatoes,
Two teaspoons of salt,
One and one-half teaspoons of paprika,
One-fourth pound of cheese, cut in small pieces,
Eight tablespoons of flour dissolved in
One-half cup of water,
Four onions, chopped fine.

Bring to a boil and cook slowly for ten minutes.

TO MAKE NOODLES

Break into a mixing bowl one egg and then add

Three tablespoons of water,
One-half teaspoon of salt,
Pinch of pepper.

Beat to mix and then add sufficient flour to make a stiff dough. Knead for five minutes and then cover and let stand for ten minutes. Now roll out on a floured pastry board until thin as paper. Roll as for jelly and then cut into thin strips with a sharp knife. Spread out to dry for one-half hour.

GNOCCHI DI LEMOLINA

Place one cup of water and one cup of milk in a saucepan and bring to a boil. Add slowly seven tablespoons wheat cereal. Cook for ten minutes and stir constantly. Now add

One well-beaten egg.
One-half teaspoon of salt.

Beat well to mix and then pour into loaf-shaped pan to mould. When firm turn out on the moulding board and cut into blocks. Place in a well-greased baking dish; sprinkle with grated cheese and dot tiny bits of butter. Bake in a hot oven until the cheese forms a light brown crust. Serve with tomato sauce.

MACARONI SOUFFLÉ

Cook one-fourth pound of macaroni and then cool and chop fine. Place in a bowl and add

One onion, chopped fine,
One red pepper, chopped fine,
Four bunches parsley, chopped fine,
Yolks of two eggs,
Two cups of cream sauce,
One and one-half teaspoon of salt,
One teaspoon of paprika.

Beat to mix and then cut and fold in the stiffly beaten whites of two eggs. Pour into a greased baking dish and bake in a moderate oven for twenty minutes. Serve at once.

RICE

Rice is extensively cultivated in the Orient and supplies the principal food to nearly one-half the population of the entire world. There is every reason why rice should be a daily article of diet in planning the menu. It is more nutritious than the potato and it digests more readily. When properly cooked and served it is an ideal starchy food.

Unpolished rice contains all the nutritions of the grains, which is approximately 6 per cent. fat, 8 per cent. protein, 79 per cent. carbohydrates. The polished variety contains an average of 88 per cent. nutrition. Polished rice has been robbed of its vital life-giving elements.

Rice is graded for size and condition and then prepared for the trade. It is known as fancy head rice, choice, prime, good, medium, common and screenings. Patna rice, the small slender, well-rounded grain, is in great demand in the East, with the Japan, Siam, Java, Rangoon, and Passein varieties closely following. In this country the Carolina, Japan and Honduras are popularly in demand.

The Carolina rice is a large sweet-flavored grain of good color and appearance. Japanese rice is a thick-bodied, soft-grained variety. Honduras variety is the slender, well-shaped grain.

The preparation of rice for the markets involves, first, the threshing, and second, the milling, which removes the husks, and, third, the polishing to produce the pearly white gloss which so many folks think is very desirable.

Polished rice has been robbed of nearly all its fat and mineral content, and thus its food value is lowered and it is deprived of its flavor.

The rice dishes, as prepared in the Oriental countries, are made from fancy unpolished head rice and they form some of the main dishes.

The Oriental first washes his rice in several waters, rubbing it vigorously between the hands. This thoroughly cleanses it. Now, to follow this method, have a saucepan containing boiling water and then add the rice slowly, so that the water continually boils. Cook until tender and then remove the lid from the saucepan and cover the rice with a cloth to absorb the moisture.

Set in a warm place for five minutes. This will give the saucepan containing a mass of delicious, fluffy rice, each grain distinct and separate.

Now, if you carefully measure both your rice and then the water, it will not be necessary for you to drain off the excess water and thus lose the valuable mineral and fat content.

HOW TO COOK RICE AMERICAN STYLE

Place in a double boiler two and one-half cups of boiling water and then add one teaspoon of salt. Now add slowly one-half cup of well-washed, unpolished rice. Cover and cook until the rice is tender and the water absorbed. Remove the lid and then cover the rice closely with a clean napkin and cook for five minutes. This will fluff each grain of rice.

It is now ready to serve, either as a vegetable to replace the potato or prepared into many delectable dishes that our Oriental neighbors relish so keenly.

JAPANESE RICE

Wash and chop fine two medium-sized leeks and then cook tender in one-half cup of water. Drain. Now add

Two cups of cooked rice,
One teaspoon of salt,
One teaspoon of soy.

Mix thoroughly and then dish on a hot baking dish. Cover with slices of hard-boiled eggs. Sprinkle with finely chopped parsley and garnish with slices of smoked salmon. Place in the oven for a few minutes to heat. Soy may be purchased at fancy grocers.

INDIAN RICE

Add three cups of cooked rice to

One quart of chicken stock,

One onion, grated fine,
One and one-half teaspoons of salt,
One-half teaspoon of paprika,
One-half teaspoon of curry powder.

Cook fifteen minutes, and serve very hot, garnish with finely chopped parsley.

CREOLE RICE

Chop one large onion and one green pepper fine, and then place in a saucepan and add

One cup of canned tomatoes rubbed through a sieve,
One-half cup of cold boiled ham chopped fine.

Cook slowly for ten minutes and then add

Three cups of cooked rice,
Two teaspoons of salt,
One teaspoon of paprika.

Mix thoroughly and then heat until very hot and serve. Cold roast pork may be used to replace the ham.

ITALIAN RICE

Place three tablespoons of vegetable cooking oil in a frying pan and add four tablespoons of well-washed rice. Toss until the rice is well brown and then add

One and one-half cups of boiling water,
Three onions, chopped fine,
One green pepper, chopped fine,
One cup of strained canned tomatoes.

Cook until the rice is soft and then add

Two teaspoons of salt,
One and one-half teaspoons of paprika,
One-half cup of grated cheese.

Stir until well blended and then serve, garnished with finely chopped parsley.

BELGIAN RICE BALLS

Place two cups of cooked rice in a bowl and add

One-half cup of currants,
One-half cup of sugar,
One well beaten egg,
One teaspoon of vanilla.

Mix and then form into small balls, about the size of an orange. Dip into beaten egg and then roll in fine bread crumbs. Fry until golden brown in hot fat. Serve with crushed and sweetened fruit.

SWEDISH RICE PUDDING

Place in a baking dish

One quart of milk,
Six tablespoons of well-washed rice,
Two-thirds cup of sugar,
One teaspoon of vanilla extract,
One-half teaspoon of salt,
Two tablespoons of butter, broken into tiny balls.

Bake in a slow oven for one hour and stir two or three times.

The cultivation of rice in Louisiana is more than a hundred years old. Louisiana now produces a crop of this cereal larger than the entire crop of the states of Georgia and Carolina. The tourist who visits Louisiana during the time of the rice market enjoys a scene that is rarely duplicated elsewhere in the civilized world; for here are gathered the buyers from all parts of the country.

The Creole of Louisiana, like the Oriental, has the true secret for making this food a palatable article of diet. The old mammy in New Orleans always tells her children that, of course, le riz must be thoroughly washed and she always insists that the grains be cleansed in four waters—two warm and two cold—and then it is cooked in the same manner as the Orientals use.

Never stir the rice while it is cooking; this will make it mushy. Instead, always shake the sauce-pan. Never flood the rice with water while it is cooking. Always keep the fact in mind that just five times the actual measurements of the rice in water will be required to cook it.

In this way there will be no excess water to drain off. So if you are using one-quarter cup of rice you would use one and one-quarter cups of water. Now you cannot pile up the water; you must be accurate in measuring the rice.

Boiled rice is a delicious accompaniment to chicken, lamb, turkey, shrimp, crabs and lobster—with okra and for oyster, chicken and crab grumbo; as a vegetable to replace potatoes and as a border for stews, goulashes, etc.

PIMENTO SANDWICHES

Use one tall or two small cans of pimentos.

One cup of cottage cheese,
One onion.

Put the pimento, cheese and onion through the food-chopper and then add four tablespoons of salad dressing and use for sandwich filling.

BAKED APPLES

Pare and core apples and then place in muffin pans and add

Two tablespoons of syrup,

One tablespoon of water,
One-quarter teaspoon of nutmeg.

Bake in a moderate oven until the apples are tender and then cool. To serve: Lift the apples into a small platter and cover with a fruit meringue and then sprinkle with cocoanut.

SPICED APPLES

Place six medium-sized apples in a casserole and then add

One piece of stick cinnamon, broken into pieces,
Four cloves,
Two allspice,
Two blades of mace,
One-half teaspoon of nutmeg,
Three-quarters cup of brown sugar,
One-half cup of cider.

Bake until tender and then serve cold.

CALAS

The old negro women of the old French quarters in New Orleans used to make a delicious rice cake, which they carried in bowls on their heads. The bowls were covered with an immaculately clean cloth and the cakes were called bella cala—tout chaud of New Orleans.

HOW TO MAKE THIS DELICIOUS RICE CAKE

(Use Level Measurements)

Wash one-half cup of rice and cook until tender in two and one-half cups of boiling water. Now cool and mash the rice well. Now dissolve one-half yeast cake in one-half cup of water 80 degrees Fahrenheit and pour into a bowl, and add

One-half teaspoon of salt,

Four tablespoons of sugar,
One-half cup of sifted flour,
The mashed rice.

Beat well to mix and then cover and let rise over night. In the morning add

Two well-beaten eggs,
Five tablespoons of sugar,
Four tablespoons of flour,
One teaspoon of nutmeg.

Beat well and then let rise for three-quarters of an hour in a warm room. Now place in the pan one and one-half cups of vegetable oil. Heat until hot enough to brown a crust of bread while you count forty. Drop the rice mixture in by the spoonful and fry until golden brown. Lift to a soft paper to drain. Dish on a hot platter; cover with warm napkin. Dust with pulverized sugar and nutmeg.

APPLE AND RICE CUSTARD

Wash six tablespoons or two ounces of rice in several waters and then place in a saucepan and add two cupsful of boiling water. Cook until the water is absorbed and the rice soft. Now wash, then cut into small pieces four small apples and then cover the apples with cold water and cook until soft. Rub through a fine sieve and add

One-half cup of sugar,
One teaspoon of vanilla,
One well-beaten egg,
The cooked rice.

Beat to mix and then pour into the custard cups and bake for fifteen minutes in a moderate oven.

SARDINE SANDWICHES

Open a box of sardines and then drain free from oil. Remove the skin and bone and then mash very fine. Add

Two hard-boiled eggs,
One green pepper,
One-quarter onion.

Chop all fine and mix to a paste with six tablespoons of salad dressing, one-half teaspoon of salt and one teaspoon of paprika.

Spread between the prepared bread and then cut into two pieces. Wrap in wax-paper until needed.

MY IDEAL APPLE SAUCE

Wash one-quarter peck of apples and then cut in pieces and place in a saucepan and add three cups of water.

Cook until soft and then rub through a fine sieve. Sweeten with

One cup of sugar,
One-half teaspoon of nutmeg,
One teaspoon of vanilla.

If red apples are used, this makes a most delicious pink-looking sauce. No need to peal or core apples.

APPLE CROQUETTES

Wash and cut into small pieces six medium-sized apples and then place in a saucepan and add one cup of water; cook slowly until the apples are soft, and then rub through a fine sieve and add

One-half cup of brown sugar,
One teaspoon of nutmeg,
One teaspoon of grated rind of lemon,
Two and one-half cups of bread crumbs,
One-half cupful of finely chopped raisins.

Mix thoroughly and then mould into croquettes and roll in flour, then fry until golden brown in hot fat. Serve with a custard sauce.

SALMON SANDWICHES

Open and drain a can of salmon and then remove the skin and bones. Place the salmon in a bowl and add

One onion, grated,
One-quarter cup of finely chopped parsley,
One-half cup of salad dressing,
Juice of one-half lemon.

Mix and then prepare the bread. Place a leaf of lettuce on the bread and then spread the prepared filling, season and place the top slice of bread in position and cut into triangles.

ORANGES

The first orange crop of the season usually reaches the market about the end of October. The early Floridas are first, and they are closely followed by the Arizona navels, and just before Christmas comes the bulk of California and Florida oranges.

ORANGE SYRUP

Grate very lightly the rind from one dozen oranges and then place three pounds of sugar and the grated rind and the juice of oranges in a clean aluminum saucepan. Place where it will heat very slowly and then the sugar will melt. Stir frequently and do not let it boil. Cover closely and then strain into sterilized bottles. Place the bottles in a hot-water bath and process for forty minutes. Place the corks in the bottles and when cool dip in melted sealing wax. This recipe may be divided. To be used for making drinks, sauces, etc.

ORANGE JUICE

Place in a bowl

Juice of twenty-five oranges,
Grated rind of ten oranges,

One pound sugar

and then allow to stand for three hours. Strain and fill into sterilized bottles and process for forty minutes in a hot-water bath. Cork, and then finish like orange syrup.

Note.—Soak the cork in boiling water for one hour to soften. This will permit you to use a slightly larger cork and insure a good closing.

To use orange syrup: Place four tablespoons in a glass and then fill with carbonated water.

To use orange juice for making orangeade, dilute with equal parts of water and juice and chill, then serve.

SCOTCH ORANGE MARMALADE

Cut twelve oranges in half and then with a sharp knife cut into thin paper-like slices and remove all the seeds. Place in a preserving kettle and add five pints of cold water. Set aside for twelve hours and then bring to a boil and cook until the fruit is tender. Add the juice of four lemons and five cups of apple sauce and then bring to a boil and measure. Add three-quarters cup of sugar for every cup of mixture. Return to the kettle and bring to a boil. Cook until it forms a very thick jam, or until 223 degrees Fahrenheit is reached on the candy thermometer.

ORANGE PRESERVE IN SYRUP

Pare and separate nine oranges into sections, taking care to break as little as possible. Now place

Two pints of water,
Four pounds of sugar

in a preserving kettle and bring to a boil. Cook for fifteen minutes and then add the oranges and cook until the oranges are tender. Lift the oranges into a jar and bring the syrup to a boil. Pour over the fruit and then seal and store in a cool, dry place. Any syrup left over may be used on cereal or hot cakes.

ORANGE SALAD

Remove the peel from four oranges and then separate the carpels and cut with a sharp scissors into pieces. Place in a bowl and add

One cup of cocoanut.

Toss the bowl gently to coat the fruit with the cocoanut and then fill into a nest of salad, and serve with orange dressing.

ORANGE SOUFFLÉ

Juice of three oranges,
One-half cup of water,
One-half cup of sugar,
Five level tablespoons of cornstarch.

Dissolve the starch and sugar in the water and then add the juice and bring to a boil. Cook for five minutes and then cool. Now add the

Yolks of two eggs,
One orange cut in tiny pieces.

Beat to mix and then carefully cut and fold in the stiffly beaten whites of two eggs. Pour into a well-buttered soufflé dish and set in a pan of warm water. Bake in a moderate oven until firm in the centre. Serve warm, with orange syrup for a sauce.

ORANGE CREAM PIE

Line a pie tin with plain pastry and then place in a saucepan

One cup of milk,
One-half cup of water,
Juice of three oranges,
Grated rind of one-half orange,
Six level tablespoons of cornstarch,
Three-quarters cup of sugar.

Dissolve the cornstarch and the sugar in the water and add the milk and fruit juice. Bring to a boil and cook for five minutes, partly cool and then add

One whole egg,
Yolk of one egg.

Beat to thoroughly blend and then pour into prepared tins and bake in a very slow oven for thirty minutes. Cool and cover with a fruit meringue, using one-half glass of orange marmalade and the white of one egg, beaten until it forms a very stiff meringue.

ORANGE AND RICE CUSTARD

Wash one-half cup of rice and then cook until tender in three cups of water and the water is absorbed. Now add

Grated rind of one orange,
Three oranges cut in tiny pieces,
Three-quarters cup of sugar.

Mix thoroughly and then place in a bowl

Two cups of milk,
Yolks of two eggs.

Beat to mix and then pour over the prepared rice. Mix thoroughly and then pour in either individual custard cups or into a baking dish. Set in a pan of warm water and then bake for thirty minutes in a moderate oven. Cool and serve with orange whip.

One glass of orange marmalade,
Whites of two eggs.

Beat with a Dover egg-beater until very stiff and then pile on rice.

SPICED PRUNES

Prepare one pound of prunes for cooking and then place in a casserole dish and add

One cup of water,
One-quarter cup of vinegar,
One cup of brown sugar,
One piece of stick cinnamon,
Six cloves,
Four allspice,
Two blades of mace,
One-half teaspoon of nutmeg.

Cook slowly until the prunes are tender and then drain the syrup and boil ten minutes before pouring over the prunes. Serve cold as a condiment with meat.

ORANGE DRESSING

Juice of two oranges,
Grated rind of one-half of an orange,
One-half cup of cold water,
One-half cup of sugar,
Two tablespoons of cornstarch.

Dissolve the sugar and the starch in water and add the fruit juice and the grated rind. Bring to a boil and cook for five minutes, and then remove from the fire and drop in yolk of one egg. Beat well to mix. Now beat the white very stiff, and then beat into the mixture and then chill and serve.

ORANGE BETTY

Pare and cut into dice three oranges. Place in a bowl and add

One and one-half cups of fine bread crumbs,
One cup of boiling water.

Mix, let cool, and then add

One well-beaten egg,
Three-quarters cup of milk,
Three tablespoons of shortening,
One-half cup of syrup,
One-half cup of sugar,
Three teaspoons of baking powder,
Six tablespoons of flour.

Mix thoroughly and then pour into either individual custard cups or into a pudding mould and set in a pan of hot water. If the Betty is put in custard cups, grease them well and bake for forty minutes in a moderate oven. If put into a mould, bake for one hour.

ORANGE FRITTERS

Pare three oranges and then with a sharp knife cut into one-half inch slices. Dip the slices in flour, then into a batter, and fry until golden brown in hot fat.

THE BATTER

Break one egg in a cup land then fill with milk. Place in a bowl and add

One and one-half cups of flour,
Two teaspoons of baking powder,
One-quarter teaspoon of salt,
Two tablespoons of sugar.

Serve orange fritters with orange dressing or orange syrup.

BAKED PRUNES

Prepare one-half pound of prunes for cooking and place in a casserole dish. Add one-half of an orange cut in thin paper-like slices. Cover the dish and place in an oven to bake very slowly. Now if the prunes are soaked early in the morning and then prepared for baking and placed in the oven when the fire is slacked off for the night, they will be done very nicely in the morning. This long, slow cooking is just what the prune requires.

PRUNE SALAD

Prepare the prunes as for stuffing and then place one-half cup of cottage cheese in a bowl and add

One green pepper chopped fine,
One-half teaspoon of salt,
One-half teaspoon of paprika.

Blend thoroughly and then fill into the pitted prunes. Now arrange the stuffed prunes upon crisp lettuce leaves and sprinkle with lemon juice. Serve with either paprika or mayonnaise dressing. This is very nice for luncheon or supper served as a salad.

CALIFORNIA PRUNE CAKE

One cup of sugar,
Six tablespoons of shortening.

Cream well until light and creamy and then add

Yolks of two eggs,
One cup of water,
Two and three-quarters cups of flour,
Two level tablespoons of baking powder,
One level tablespoon of mace.

Beat to thoroughly blend and then fold in the stiffly beaten whites of the two eggs. Now line a cake pan with greased paper and pour in a layer of the cake batter. Spread evenly. Now spread a layer of finely chopped nuts and then a layer of well-drained and cooked prunes that have been chopped fine. Cover with a layer of the cake batter and then repeat this until the pan, is three-quarters full. Then dust the top of the cake lightly with sugar. Place in a moderate oven and bake for one hour. Cool, and then ice with icing made of

Three-quarters cup of XXXX sugar,
One tablespoon of lemon juice,

and sufficient boiling water to moisten. Then spread on the cake.

PRUNE AND NUT JELLY

Soak three level tablespoons of gelatine in one-half cup of cold water for one-half hour. Now stone sufficient prunes to measure one cup. Add

One-half cup of finely chopped nuts,
One-half cup of sugar,
One cup of prune juice,
Juice of one lemon.

Now place the gelatine in a hot-water bath and then strain into the prune mixture. Stir until thoroughly mixed and then pour into moulds. Set aside to mould and then serve with fruit whip.

PRUNE DELICACIES

Wash the prunes thoroughly and then drain and turn on a cloth to dry. Remove the stones and fill the centres with a mixture of chopped nuts and ginger. Roll in granulated sugar. Prunes may be filled with fondant or fudge.

PRUNE CHARLOTTE

Soak three level tablespoons of gelatine in one-half cup of cold water for one-half hour. Then set in hot water bath to melt. Strain into a bowl and add

One cup of prune juice,
Juice of one lemon,
One-half cup of sugar.

Heat to dissolve sugar and then cool before adding to the gelatine. Now place a few spoonfuls of the prepared gelatine mixture in a mould and turn to thoroughly coat the mould. Then line the mould with cooked and stoned prunes. Pour a few spoonfuls of the gelatine mixture over the prunes and set them in place before pouring in the remainder of the mixture; then set aside to mould. When ready to serve unmould on platter and serve with prune sauce.

One cup of prune juice,
Juice of one lemon,
Six tablespoons of sugar.

Heat to dissolve sugar and then cool before serving.

RHUBARB

To cook rhubarb, cut it into inch pieces and remove the stringy peel. Cook in a glass or earthen casserole dish in the oven until it is soft, adding just enough sugar to sweeten. This will give you a splendid product.

Do not use the leaves of the rhubarb. And do not cook rhubarb in tin; the mineral salt or acid content of the fruit reacts upon the metal and sets up an active poison.

TO COOK RHUBARB FOR PIES

Prepare the rhubarb and then sprinkle well with flour and add sugar, and cook slowly until tender. The flour will thicken the mixture. Then pour into the prepared pie plate and cover with pastry. Bake in a moderate oven for twenty minutes. Pie made in this way will be far superior to that made where the rhubarb is cut and placed in the pie and then cooked.

RHUBARB AND RAISIN CONSERVE

Wash and peel and then cut the rhubarb into one-half inch pieces. Measure one quart of the cut pieces and place in a baking dish, adding

One cup of seeded raisins,
Two cups of sugar.

Do not add water; cover and cook until the fruit is tender, usually about forty minutes.

RHUBARB FRUIT SAUCE

Place the whites of two eggs in a bowl and then add one-half glass of jelly. Beat until very stiff and then add one cup of very thick rhubarb sauce.

RHUBARB SHORTCAKE

Place two cups of flour in a bowl and add

One teaspoon of salt,
Four teaspoons of baking powder,
One-half cup of sugar.

Sift to mix and then rub in six tablespoons of shortening. Mix to a dough with two-thirds cup of milk. Cut with a large cookie cutter and then bake in a hot oven for fifteen minutes. Split and butter, and then fill with the cooked rhubarb and serve with either plain or whipped cream or custard sauce.

RHUBARB COCKTAIL

Place three tablespoons of rhubarb conserve in a cocktail glass. Add layer of thinly sliced bananas and then a layer of shredded orange. Sprinkle with powdered sugar and top with whipped cream or stiffly beaten white of egg. Garnish with maraschino cherries.

RHUBARB PUFFS

Three-quarters cup of sugar,
One-half cup of water,
Five tablespoons of shortening.

Place in a bowl and then add

One egg,
Two cups of flour,
Four teaspoons of baking powder,
One-half teaspoon of salt,
One cup of finely chopped rhubarb (raw).

Beat to mix and then fill into well-greased custard cups and bake for thirty minutes in a hot oven.

VERMONT RHUBARB GRIDDLE CAKES

Soak stale bread in cold water to soften. Press very dry and then rub through a fine sieve. Now measure two cups and place in a bowl and add

One and one-half cups of sweetened rhubarb,
One egg,
One and three-quarters cups of sifted flour,
Four teaspoons of baking powder,
One teaspoon of salt,
One tablespoon of shortening.

Mix well and then bake on a griddle and serve with sugar, cinnamon and butter or syrup.

RHUBARB GELATINE

Two cups of cold, cooked and sweetened rhubarb.

Add

Four level tablespoons of gelatine,
Juice of one orange,
One-half cup of water.

Add the gelatine to the mixture and then set aside for one-half hour to soften. Then heat slowly until the boiling point is reached, remove from the fire and pour into moulds. Let set until firm and then unmould and serve with whipped cream. Use a china or earthenware mould.

RHUBARB AND TAPIOCA PUDDING

Wash one-half cup of pearl tapioca in plenty of water to remove the starch. Place in a glass or earthenware baking dish and add four cups of cooked and sweetened rhubarb. Cook in the oven until the tapioca is transparent or soft. Place a meringue made of the white of one egg on top. Cool, and then serve.

RHUBARB DUMPLINGS

Roll the pastry out one-quarter inch thick and then cut into four-inch squares. Fill with pieces of rhubarb cut in one-half inch pieces, adding 2 tablespoons sugar. Fold the dough over, pressing it tightly, and then brush with egg-wash and bake in a slow oven for thirty minutes.

GINGER JELLY

Soak one-half package of gelatine in one cupful of cold water for thirty minutes and then add

Juice of one lemon,
One orange,
One-half cup of sugar,
One cup of boiling water.

Beat thoroughly to mix and then let cool. Just before it begins to thicken stir in one-half cup of finely chopped candied ginger.

GINGER CREAM

Soak one-half box of gelatine in one and one-half cups of cold milk for one-half hour. Now add one-half cup of sugar and set in a pan of warm water. Stir until gelatine is dissolved and then set aside to cool. While cooling place

White of one egg,
One-half glass of jelly

in a bowl and beat with a Dover egg-beater until light and fluffy. Add one-half cup of finely shredded candied ginger and then cooled gelatine. Whip until it begins to thicken and then pour into moulds to become firm.

Note.—Do not add the gelatine mixture to the fruit whip until just before it thickens.

GINGER DELICACIES

The West Indians make and serve many delicious desserts and conserves made with ginger. Either the prepared ginger in pots may be used or the ordinary ginger root may be obtained from the grocery shops. Ask for stem ginger, as this kind is less apt to be stringy and coarse.

To prepare: Soak the ginger in warm water over night and then in the morning wash, using a vegetable brush. Now scrape well and then place in fresh water enough to cover—and cook gently on the back of the stove until tender. Or it may be placed in the fireless cooker over night. When the root is tender, place

Three cupfuls of sugar,
Three-quarters cup of water,
Juice of one lemon

in a saucepan and bring to a boil. Cook for ten minutes and then add the ginger. Now place where it will just keep warm and simmer until the syrup is absorbed. Remove and stand in a cool place for two days. Reheat and then drain on a sieve and roll in sugar. Pack in an air-tight tin box and the ginger will keep indefinitely.

PINEAPPLE MOUSSE

Drain and mince sufficient pineapple fine to measure two cups. Put through a fine sieve and then place in a bowl; place whites of two eggs in a second bowl and add one glass of apple jelly. Beat until very stiff. Whip one cup of cream stiff and add one-half cup of sugar. Gently combine the fruit whip, whipped cream and puree of pineapple by cutting and folding until well mixed. Pour into two-quart mould and cover with wax paper; then place on the lid, and use one pint of salt to two and one-half pints of finely crushed ice, to set the mousse to freeze.

TO STUFF DATES WITH GINGER

Remove the stones from the dates and then fill the centre With a piece of candied ginger. Press firmly and then roll between the hands to restore to shape of date. Roll the finished date in granulated sugar. Prunes may be used to replace the dates.

EGGLESS MAYONNAISE

Place in soup plate

Two tablespoons evaporated milk,
One-half teaspoon mustard,
One-half teaspoon paprika.

Blend by beating with fork and when smooth add slowly three-quarters cup of salad oil. Beat hard for few minutes. Now add

One teaspoon sugar,
One teaspoon salt,
One teaspoon vinegar.

Then beat again until thoroughly mixed.

COOKED SALAD DRESSING

One-half cup of vinegar,
Three-quarters cup of water,
Three level tablespoons of cornstarch.

Dissolve the starch in the water and add the vinegar and bring to a boil. Cook for three minutes and then remove, and add

One egg,
One teaspoon of salt,
One teaspoon of paprika,
Three-quarters teaspoon of mustard,
One teaspoon of sugar.

Beat to mix and then beat in one cup of sour cream. This dressing may be used on potatoes, chicken and celery salad and with cold meat or plain lettuce.

FROZEN LEMON CUSTARD

Place in a saucepan

One quart of milk,
One-half cup of cornstarch.

Stir until dissolved and then bring to a boil. Cook for ten minutes. Remove from the fire and add

Three well-beaten eggs.

Beat to thoroughly mix, then cool. Now grate the rind lightly from one lemon. Place in a bowl and add

Juice of three lemons,
Juice of one orange,
One and one-half cups of sugar.

Blend well and when ready to freeze beat the lemon mixture into the custard. Add the lemon mixture very slowly. Freeze in the usual manner, using three parts of ice to one of salt. Pack, and then set aside for two hours to ripen.

GINGER-ALE SALAD

Soak four tablespoons of gelatine in four tablespoons of cold water for twenty minutes. Now add to the gelatine one-half cup of boiling ginger-ale. Stir until gelatine is dissolved and then strain. Add the balance of the one pint bottle of ginger-ale. Let cool, and then rinse off mould in ice water to thoroughly chill, and then coat the mould with the gelatine by pouring in about one-quarter cup and turning the mould until it is thoroughly coated. Now place pieces of preserved ginger in designs in the bottom of the mould, also using a few maraschino cherries. Pour a little gelatine over this and then when firm pour in sufficient gelatine to form a layer. Repeat this until the mould is filled. In warm weather pack the mould in salt and ice mixture for quick results.

EGG SALAD

Shred one head of lettuce very fine and then place in a bowl and add

One onion,
One green pepper, chopped very fine,
One cooked carrot, diced,
One cup of mayonnaise.

Mix and then garnish with four hard-boiled eggs, cut in slices. Dust with paprika.

THOUSAND ISLAND DRESSING

One-half cup salad oil,
Juice of one lemon,
Juice of one orange,
One-half green pepper, chopped fine,
One-half medium sized onion, chopped fine,
Two teaspoons salt,
One teaspoon paprika,
One-half teaspoon mustard,
One pimento chopped fine.

Blend well.

SALAD DRESSING

To make mayonnaise dressing, break one egg in a bowl and then add

Two teaspoons of vinegar,
One teaspoon of sugar,
One teaspoon of paprika,
One-half teaspoon of mustard.

Beat with Dover beater to mix and then have some one pour in slowly one cup of oil while you beat the mixture with a steady motion.

CUCUMBER SALAD

Pare the cucumbers and then cut into thin slices and cover with two tablespoons of salt and cracked ice for one hour. Wash and then drain. Now shred fine the coarse green leaves of the lettuce. Arrange the cucumbers on the prepared lettuce and serve with sour cream dressing.

FRUIT SALAD

Pare and cut into dice

Two oranges,
Two apples,
Three bananas.

Place in a bowl and add one cup of cocoanut and toss gently to mix. Now place in a nest of lettuce. Prepare a fruit salad dressing of

One cup of sugar,
One cup of water,
Juice of one orange,
Juice of one lemon,
Three level tablespoons of cornstarch.

Dissolve the sugar and starch and bring to a boil. Cook for five minutes and then remove from the fire, and add yolk of one egg. Beat hard to mix and then fold in the stiffly beaten white of one egg. Cool, and then pour over the fruit salad. Garnish with maraschino cherries. This amount of salad will serve eight persons.

COLESLAW

Shred a head of cabbage fine and place in salted water for one-half hour. Drain well and then add

Two green peppers, chopped fine,
One cup of mayonnaise,
One tablespoon of salt,
One tablespoon of paprika,
One-quarter cup of vinegar.

Mix.

SALMON SALAD

Open a can of salmon and then drain and remove the bones and add

Two green peppers, chopped fine,
One onion, chopped fine.

Mix, shred the coarse outer green leaves of the lettuce fine and then line a bowl with crisp lettuce. Place the shredded lettuce in the nest and then the prepared salmon. Serve with sliced hard-boiled egg and mayonnaise dressing.

POACHED EGGS ON FRENCH TOAST

Trim the crust from slices of bread and then dip in the following:

One cup of milk,
One egg.

Beat to mix and then fry the bread until golden brown in hot fat. Poach the eggs and then lift on a napkin to drain. Then roll gently on the French toast. Cover with a cream sauce and garnish with finely shredded parsley.

PICKLED EGGS

Hard boil one-half dozen eggs. Cook until tender one bunch of beets. Turn into a pan of cold water and then remove the skins and cut into thick slices. Place in a dish and add four large onions, cut in thin slices. Now place in a saucepan

Four tablespoons of sugar,
One teaspoon of salt,
One-half teaspoon of paprika,
One cup of vinegar,
One-half cup of water.

Bring to a boil and cook for ten minutes. Pour over the beets. Add the hard-boiled eggs.

OMELET

Place the yolks of three eggs in a bowl and add

Two tablespoons of milk,
One-half cup of prepared bread crumbs,
Two tablespoons of finely minced parsley,
One teaspoon of salt,
One-half teaspoon of pepper.

Mix and then cut and fold in the stiffly beaten whites of three eggs and then place four tablespoons of shortening in a frying pan. When fat is smoking hot pour in the omelet and cook gently until firm, then turn either by lifting or rolling, using the cake-turner or a spatula, or it can be turned into another hot pan, containing one tablespoon of shortening, then fold and roll.

How to prepare the bread: Soak stale bread in hot water to soften and then place in a cloth and squeeze very dry.

DEVILED EGGS, PARISIENNE

Boil one egg hard for each person, cut in half, cutting the length of the egg. Rub the yolks through a fine sieve into a bowl and then add to every six eggs

One-half cup of finely chopped ham,
One onion, grated,
One green pepper, chopped fine,
One and one-half teaspoons of salt,

One teaspoon of paprika,
One-half teaspoon of mustard,
Six tablespoons of mayonnaise dressing.

Mix and then fill back into the whites of the eggs. Mould up very high and then roll in finely grated cheese and dust with paprika. Roll in wax-paper. Set in ice-box until ready to serve.

BAKED OMELET

Place in a bowl

Yolks of four eggs,
One cup of thick cream sauce,
One teaspoon of salt,
One-half teaspoon of paprika,
Two tablespoons of finely chopped parsley.

Beat to mix thoroughly and then cut and fold in the stiffly beaten whites of four eggs. Pour in a baking or casserole dish and bake in a moderate oven until firm in the centre. Garnish with strips of bacon and serve with cheese sauce.

To make cheese sauce: Place three tablespoons of grated cheese in a cup of cream sauce.

MORAVIAN OMELET

Soak one-half cup of sifted stale bread crumbs in one-half cup of milk, adding

One-half teaspoon of salt,
One-quarter teaspoon of pepper,
One teaspoon of grated onion,
One tablespoon of finely minced parsley,
Three well-beaten eggs.

Mix thoroughly and then heat four tablespoons of shortening in a frying pan until smoking hot and then pour in the mixture. Reduce the heat and cook until set. Fold and turn and then roll. Turn on a hot platter. This amount will serve two persons.

CHEESE CUTLETS

Place in a saucepan

One and one-half cups of milk,
Nine level tablespoons of flour.

Stir to dissolve the flour and then bring to a boil. Cook for two minutes and then add

One-quarter pound of cheese, cut fine.

Stir until the cheese is melted and then remove from the fire and add

One small onion grated,
One teaspoon of paprika,
One and one-half teaspoons of salt.

Turn on a greased platter and set to cool. Mould. It takes about four hours to become firm enough to mould into cutlets. Mould into shape and then roll in flour and dip in beaten egg, then in fine crumbs and fry until golden brown in hot fat. Garnish with watercress.

COUNTRY CHEESE SANDWICHES

Place one cup of country or buttermilk cheese in a bowl and add

One-half cup of thick mayonnaise,
One onion, chopped very fine,
One green pepper, chopped very fine,
Two teaspoons of salt,
Two teaspoons of paprika,
One-half teaspoon mustard.

Mix thoroughly and then spread the rye bread with English butter, and then spread the filling between the slices of bread and cut into finger-width strips.

CHEESE SANDWICHES

Place in a bowl

One-half cup of grated cheese, and then add
One tablespoon of grated onion,
Two tablespoons of finely minced green peppers,
One teaspoon of salt,
One teaspoon of paprika,
One-half teaspoon of mustard,
Six tablespoons of mayonnaise dressing.

Mix thoroughly and then spread between the bread as prepared for bread and butter sandwiches.

A FEW POINTERS ABOUT VEGETABLES

Do not oversalt vegetables. Never salt while cooking; too much salt not only toughens the delicate fibres but also neutralizes the valuable mineral content.

Add just sufficient boiling water to cover and then bring to a boil. Then cook slowly until tender. Do not cover the saucepan in which the vegetables are cooking. This condenses the steam which contains the volatile oils and thus darkens the vegetable.

PUREE OF PEAS

Rub one cup of cooked peas through a sieve and add

One cup of milk,
One-half cup of water,
One tablespoon of cornstarch,
One teaspoon of grated onions,

One teaspoon of finely chopped parsley.

Dissolve the starch in the water and add the balance of the ingredients to the pea puree. Bring to a boil and cook for five minutes. Season with salt and pepper and serve with croutons or toast, slices of bread cut in half-inch blocks.

PEA SOUFFLE

Place in a bowl

One cup of thick cream sauce,

and then rub

Four tablespoons of cooked peas through a sieve.

Now add

Five tablespoons of bread crumbs,
One teaspoon of grated onion,
One-half teaspoon of salt,
One-quarter teaspoon of pepper,
Yolks of two eggs.

Beat to mix, then fold in the stiffly beaten whites of the two eggs. Pour into a greased baking dish and bake in a moderate oven until firm in the centre. Serve at once. This dish replaces meat.

PEA PUDDING

Put four tablespoons of peas through a sieve and then place in a bowl and add

One cup of thick cream sauce,
Four tablespoons of fine bread crumbs,
One well beaten egg,
One teaspoon of finely minced parsley,

One teaspoon of grated onions,
One-half teaspoon of paprika,
One-half teaspoon of salt.

Mix to blend, then pour in well-greased custard cups. Bake until firm in the centre. Serve in cups, or turn out on a slice of toast and cover with cream of hollandaise sauce.

NOTE.—Set the pudding in a pan containing warm water while baking.

BAKED DRIED CORN

Soak one and one-half cups of corn over night and then in the morning drain and place in a saucepan and cover with boiling water. Simmer slowly until tender and then drain and season with

One small onion, minced fine,
Two tablespoons of dried parsley,
One teaspoon of salt,
One-half teaspoon of white pepper.

Place in a casserole dish and cover with one and a half cups of cream sauce. Sprinkle with fine bread crumbs and one tablespoon of finely grated cheese. Bake for twenty minutes in the oven. This dish replaces meat for luncheon.

SQUASH

SQUASH AU GRATIN

Wash, pare and cut the squash into pieces, discarding the seeds. Steam until tender and then drain well and stand on the back of the range to dry. Now rub the pulp through a sieve. Measure and add to each cup of pulp

One well-beaten egg,
Two tablespoons of butter,
One teaspoon of salt,
One-half teaspoon of paprika,
Two tablespoons of milk,

One tablespoon of finely minced parsley.

Pour into well-greased baking dish and cover with fine bread crumbs and two tablespoons of grated cheese. Bake in a slow oven for twenty minutes.

SQUASH CAKES

Wash and cut the squash into pieces and then cook until tender in boiling water, then drain and rub pulp through sieve. Now measure and place in a bowl

One cup of prepared squash,
One well-beaten egg,
One tablespoon of shortening,
One-half cup of milk,
One and one-half cups of flour,
Two tablespoons of baking powder,
One-half teaspoon of salt,
One-half teaspoon of paprika,
One tablespoon of minced parsley.

Beat to mix and then bake as if for griddle cakes on a hot griddle. Serve with maple syrup.

SQUASH SOUFFLE

One cup of prepared squash pulp,
One tablespoon of grated onion,
Two tablespoons of finely minced parsley,
One tablespoon of melted butter,
Two teaspoons of salt,
One teaspoon of paprika,
One cup of very thick cream sauce,
Yolks of two eggs.

Beat to blend and then carefully fold in the stiffly beaten whites of two eggs. Pour into well-greased individual custard cups and set in a pan of warm water. Bake slowly in a moderate oven until firm in the centre, usually about twenty minutes. Let stand about three minutes after removing from the oven and then turn on a slice of toast and cover with cheese sauce and serve.

SQUASH ITALIENNE

One and one-half cups of prepared squash pulp,
One and one-half teaspoons of salt,
One teaspoon of paprika,
Two tablespoons of finely minced parsley,
Two tablespoons of finely minced onions.

Mix thoroughly and then dice two ounces of salt pork. Brown the salt pork nicely and then drain off about one-half of the fat in the pan. Turn the squash mixture on the salt pork and heat and serve.

SQUASH PIE

Wash and then cut the squash into pieces and then boil until tender and drain; rub the pulp through sieve. Measure, and to each cup add

One cup of sugar,
Two tablespoons of melted butter,
Two well-beaten eggs,
One cup of milk,
One-half teaspoon of nutmeg.

Beat well to mix and then pour in a pie tin which has been lined with plain pastry. Sprinkle one-half cup of currants over the top and bake for one-half hour in a slow oven.

BAKED SQUASH

Cut a slice from the top of the squash and remove the seeds and the string fibre. Now add

One tablespoon of melted butter,
One-half teaspoon of salt,

One-half teaspoon of paprika.

Cover closely with a lid and then bake in a slow oven until the pulp is tender, usually about thirty minutes. Remove the lip and scoop out the pulp with a spoon, piling it into a hot vegetable dish, and garnish with finely chopped parsley and then serve.

SQUASH BISCUIT

Place in a bowl

Three and one-half cups of sifted flour,
One teaspoon of salt,
Five teaspoons of baking powder.

Sift to mix and then rub in five tablespoons of shortening and mix to a dough with one cup of prepared squash pulp. Work to a dough and blend evenly, then roll out on a slightly floured board three-quarters of an inch thick. Cut and brush the tops with milk and bake in a hot oven for fifteen minutes.

Squash may be used to replace potatoes when making bread. Add one cup of squash pulp to ginger-bread, or when making small cakes it will be found to be delicious when used this way.

OMELET IN TOMATO CASES

Select firm tomatoes and then cut a slice from the tops and with a spoon carefully remove the centres. Place the tomato in well-greased custard cups and then break in a bowl four eggs; then add

Four tablespoons of water,
One teaspoon of salt,
One-half teaspoon of pepper.

Beat to mix and then fill into the prepared tomato. Sprinkle one teaspoon of fine bread crumbs on top of each tomato and add

One teaspoon of butter,
Dash of paprika.

Set the custard cups in a baking pan and place in a hot oven and bake for twenty minutes. Turn on a slice of toast and cover with cream sauce.

BAKED TOMATOES, CHELSEA

Select firm tomatoes and cut a slice from the tops and scoop out the centres with a spoon. Now grease custard cups and place the tomatoes in the cups. Now shred very fine one ounce of dried beef. Divide into the four tomatoes. Break in a mixing bowl

Two eggs.

Then add

Three-quarters cup of milk,
One-half teaspoon of salt,
One-half teaspoon of paprika,
One teaspoon of grated onion,
Two teaspoons of finely minced parsley.

Beat to mix and then chop fine the pulp from the tomatoes. Place one teaspoon of this pulp in each tomato.

TOMATOES, COUNTRY STYLE

Select smooth, firm tomatoes cut in half and then place in a deep dish. Cover with cracked ice and serve with the following dressing:

COUNTRY DRESSING

Place in a bowl

Three tablespoons of salad oil,
One tablespoon of vinegar,
One teaspoon of sugar,

One teaspoon of salt,
One-half teaspoon of white pepper,
One-quarter teaspoon of mustard.

Beat until creamy and then serve ice cold.

TOMATO FRITTERS

Select firm tomatoes and then cut in one-half inch slices. Dip in the prepared batter and then fry until golden brown. Serve with cream sauce.

How to prepare the batter: Place one egg in a bowl and add

One cup of water,
One teaspoon of salt,
One-half teaspoon of pepper.

Beat to mix and then add

Two tablespoons of grated onions,
One and one-half cups of flour,
Two teaspoons of baking powder.

Beat to a smooth batter and then dip the tomatoes into it. Fry quickly until golden brown.

SPINACH

Let us first begin with the washing of the spinach. Take your cleanser and scour out the sink and then scald it with boiling water. Now place a clean cloth over the drain and turn the spinach into the sink. Use plenty of lukewarm water to wash with. This is necessary to free these crinky little leaves from the sand and grit. Now rinse in plenty of cold water to crisp it. Shake the spinach dry and place in a deep saucepan and cover and then steam gently until tender. Do not add any water. In this manner the spinach is virtually cooked in its own juices. Now turn into a chopping bowl and chop fine and then rub through a coarse sieve and it is ready for use. You must prepare and cook the spinach early in the day, so that you will have time to properly prepare it, and then, when it is wanted, simply reheat it.

SPINACH A LA MODE

Prepare and cook the spinach as given above and then turn into a sieve and let drain, with a weight, for three hours. Now chop fine and then place one tablespoon of bacon or sausage fat in the frying pan and add

One small onion, minced very fine,
The prepared spinach.

Heat slowly until very hot and then season with salt and pepper. Lift to a hot platter and garnish with a slice of hard-boiled egg.

SPINACH PUDDING

Cook the spinach as directed in the above methods and then add

One cup of creamed sauce,
One tablespoon of grated onion,
One cup of fine bread crumbs,
One and one-half teaspoons of salt,
One teaspoon of paprika.

Mix thoroughly and then pour into well-greased baking dish and bake in a hot oven for twenty minutes.

SUNSHINE SAUCE FOR VEGETABLES

Make a cream sauce, using

One and one-half cups of milk,
Seven tablespoons of flour.

Place in a saucepan and stir until dissolved, using a fork or wire whip. Bring to a boil. Cook slowly for five minutes and then add

One and one-half teaspoons of salt,
One teaspoon of white pepper,
Two tablespoons of grated onion,
Two well-beaten eggs.

Mix thoroughly and then serve with baked peppers.

SOUFFLE OF SPINACH

Cook the spinach as directed in the method and then place one cup of spinach in a bowl and add

Yolks of two eggs,
One cup of very thick cream sauce,
One tablespoon of grated onion,
Two teaspoons of salt,
One teaspoon of paprika.

Mix thoroughly, and then carefully fold in the stiffly beaten whites of two eggs and then pour into well-greased baking dish. Bake in a moderate oven for twenty-five minutes and serve with cheese sauce in place of meat for luncheon.

SPINACH NESTS

Cook spinach as for spinach à la mode and then chop fine and mould into nests. Place on a slice of bread and then break an egg into each nest and cover with two tablespoons of well-seasoned cream sauce and one teaspoon of grated cheese. Place on a baking sheet in a moderate oven for twelve minutes and serve with cream sauce for luncheon in place of meat.

SPINACH WITH HOLLANDAISE SAUCE

Cook the spinach as given in the method and then when ready to serve, reheat and make the Hollandaise sauce as follows:

Five tablespoons of salad oil,
Three tablespoons of vinegar,

One tablespoon of water,
One teaspoon of grated onion,
One-half teaspoon of paprika.

Place in a small saucepan and bring to the boiling point, and then add the yolk of egg. Stir until thick and then add sufficient salt to taste. Pour over the spinach when ready to serve.

SPINACH BALLS

Prepare spinach as for spinach à la mode and then place in a bowl and add

One hard-boiled egg, chopped fine,
One tablespoon of grated onion,
One and one-half teaspoons of salt,
One-half teaspoon of pepper,
One tablespoon of salad oil.

Mix thoroughly and then form into balls and dip in beaten egg, and then roll in fine bread crumbs and fry until golden brown in hot fat. Serve with lamb chops.

PUREE OF SPINACH ALSACE

Rub one-half cup of spinach through a sieve and then place in a bowl and add

One cup of thick brown gravy,
One teaspoon of grated onion,
One teaspoon of salt,
One-half teaspoon of paprika,
Two tablespoons of grated cheese,
One well-beaten egg,
Five tablespoons of fine bread crumbs.

Mix and then pour into custard cups. Bake in a moderate oven eighteen minutes. This will replace meat for luncheon. Cream sauce may be used instead of gravy.

SPINACH SALAD

Prepare the spinach as for spinach à la mode and then chop fine and place in a bowl, and add

One small onion, chopped fine,
One teaspoon of salt,
One-half teaspoon of paprika.

Mix, and then pack in demi-tasse cups to mould. Turn on a bed of crisp lettuce leaves and serve with French dressing.

SPINACH A LA BOURGEOIS

To one-half cup of leftover spinach add

One tablespoon grated onion,
One cup of cream sauce,
One hard-boiled egg, chopped fine,
One teaspoon of salt,
One-half teaspoon of pepper.

Mix and then place in a baking dish and sprinkle with grated cheese. Bake in a hot oven for eighteen minutes. Serve in place of meat for luncheon.

SPINACH—SCOTCH STYLE

Place in a bowl

One cup of prepared spinach,
Three-quarters cup of thick brown gravy,
One and one-half teaspoons of salt,
One-half teaspoon of white pepper.

Beat to thoroughly mix and then pour into well-greased baking dish and sprinkle two tablespoons of grated cheese and fine bread crumbs and then bake in a hot oven for twenty minutes.

HOW TO PREPARE A STOCK POT

Select a pot that has a close-fitting lid and keep it for this purpose. The usual proportion is a one-gallon pot for a family of six. You will require one pound of bones to every quart of water, and

One large onion,
One medium sized carrot,
One medium sized turnip,
One faggot of soup herbs,
Also one and one-half pounds lean meat

to every four quarts of water or less. Have the butcher crack the bones well and then rinse them under cold water and place in the pot, together with meat and the seasoning. Add the required amount of cold water and bring to a boil. Cook very slowly for three and one-half hours. Strain the liquid and discard the bones and vegetables. Set the liquid aside to cool and remove the cake of fat when it hardens. Now place the liquid in a saucepan and boil for twenty minutes. It may now be used for stock, soups, broths, gravies and sauces.

Cover the bones in the kettle with cold water again and add any leftover gravies, bits of meat, trimmings and bones that you may have on hand. Cook slowly on the back of the range for four hours, and then strain, and to two quarts of this stock add

One can of tomatoes,
One cupful of diced carrots,
One-half cup of diced onions,
One-half cup of barley,
One cupful of diced potatoes,
One-half cup of diced turnips,
One-quarter teaspoon of powdered thyme,
Two tablespoons of finely chopped parsley,
One tablespoon of dried celery leaves.

Cook slowly for one hour for a good vegetable soup. To give the soup body, add

Three-fourths cup of flour.

Dissolved in

One cup of cold water.

Cook ten minutes and then serve.

BEAN SOUP

Soak one pint of marrow-fat or soup beans over night. In the morning wash and place in soup kettle with two quarts of water, bring to a boil, turn in colander, and let drain and rinse under cold water. Return to soup kettle and add

Four quarts of water,
One faggot soup herbs,
One teaspoon thyme,
One cup finely chopped onions,
One carrot cut in tiny dice.

Cook slowly for four hours, now mince one-half pound of salt pork fine, place in frying pan and cook slowly until nice brown; add to the bean stock, mashing beans well. Serve.

Dried peas, lima beans, soy beans and lentil soup may be prepared in the same manner.

BOUILLON

Two and one-half pounds shin beef with bone,
One stock celery,
One carrot, sliced thin,
Two onions,
One clove,
One bay leaf,
One pound veal bones.

Remove bone and cut meat in small pieces, brown quickly in hot pan, place in soup kettle, and add vegetables cut in tiny dice and three quarts of cold water; bring slowly to a boil and cook slowly for three and one-half hours; strain through napkin, season and clarify white of egg and crushed egg shell.

To clarify: Set soup aside until cold, remove fat, return to stock pot, and add white of egg, crushed egg shell and one-half cup of cold water beaten together, then bring slowly to a boil, cook for five minutes and then add one-half cup of water—lift from stove, set aside to settle and strain through piece cheesecloth.

MOCK TURTLE SOUP

One calf's head.

Clean and thoroughly wash head, removing tongue and brains.

Place the head in stock pot, then add

Five quarts cold water,
Two carrots, cut in dices,
Three-quarter cup sliced onions,
One fagot soup herbs,
One-half teaspoon sweet marjoram,
One-half teaspoon thyme,
One-half cup celery leaves.

Bring to a boil and cook slowly until meat leaves the bones, lift head; cut part head in tiny dice, using about two cups of the meat; do not add to the mock turtle yet.

Now place in frying pan

One-half cup of shortening,
Three-quarters cup of flour.

Brown flour a deep mahogany brown—add part of the stock to blend into thick sauce—bring to a boil and cook slowly for five minutes; then strain into the stock or mock turtle soup. Now add

One tablespoon salt,
One teaspoon white pepper.

Simmer few minutes, strain through cheesecloth into bowl, set aside to cool, remove fat from top; now return stock to kettle and clarify as for bouillon; to serve reheat, add the chopped calf's head meat as prepared, juice of one-half lemon, two slices lemon cut in tiny pieces, two hard-boiled eggs chopped fine.

OXTAIL SOUP

Have butcher cut tail in pieces; soak ox-tail in warm water for one-half hour. Wash and wipe dry, now roll each joint in flour, place one-half cup of shortening in soup kettle, add the ox-tails and brown well, then add one-half cup flour, browning a deep mahogany brown; now add

Three quarts cold water,
One bunch soup herbs,
Four onions chopped fine,
One carrot cut in dice,
One teaspoon of thyme.

Cook slowly for three hours, season with pepper and salt and juice of one-half lemon.

MULLIGATAWNY SOUP

Place in a saucepan

Three pints of chicken stock,
One cup diced apples,
Four onions chopped fine,
One carrot cut in dice,
One clove,

One-half teaspoon of thyme.

Simmer slowly for one-half hour.

Now place in frying pan

Four tablespoons bacon fat,
One-half cup of flour,
One-half teaspoon curry powder.

Blend together, and then add one pint of cold water, and as soon as it is thoroughly blended turn into the soup; stir to prevent lumping and bring quickly to a boil; cook ten minutes; strain through cheesecloth; add juice one-half lemon and one-half cup of finely chopped chicken meat. Serve.

FRENCH PEA SOUP

Soak one cup of dried peas over night and then in the morning drain and place in a saucepan, adding

Two quarts of water.

Simmer gently until tender and then pass through a sieve and add

Two large onions, grated,
Two tablespoons of parsley, minced fine,
Six whole cloves,
One small bay leaf,
One-half cup of strained canned tomatoes.

Simmer slowly for thirty minutes and then serve with toasted strips of bread.

FAGGOT OF SOUP HERBS

Divide one leek into three parts and cut from the stem up. To this piece of leek add

Four branches of thyme,
Two branches of parsley,
One piece of carrot, cut in a strip three inches long,
Two branches of celery,
One small pepper pod.

Tie with a string and dry in a warm place. When dry put in a glass jar to be used as needed.

Many varieties of soups may be made from the plain stock with just a few minutes' work.

Clear tomato soup: To one quart of stock add one cupful of canned tomatoes, rubbed through a fine sieve. Noodles, macaroni or any cooked vegetable may be added.

For clear soup: Add one teaspoon of kitchen bouquet and any desired vegetables to each quart of stock. When making cream soups, if you will add one cupful of prepared stock to each cup of milk, your soup will have a delicious flavor.

Stock may be made, filled into sterilized jars and then the rubber and lid adjusted; the soup may then be processed for three hours in a hot-water bath. Remove from the bath, fasten the lids securely, and then test for leaks and store in a dry cool place. Where there is a fire kept in the kitchen, it will not add to the costs to can soups, stocks, etc., for future use.

PEPPER POT

Place in a saucepan

Two calves' feet, cut in pieces,
One pound cooked honeycomb tripe, cut in small blocks,
One cup of finely chopped onions,
One bunch of soup herbs,
One teaspoon of sweet marjoram,
Two whole cloves,
Two whole allspice,

Four quarts of water.

Bring to a boil and cook slowly for three hours. Remove the calves' feet, remove meat from the fat, chop meat fine and return to soup, then add three cups of finely diced potatoes and tiny dumplings made as follows:

Place in a mixing bowl

One cup of flour,
One-half teaspoon of salt,
One-half teaspoon of pepper,
One-half teaspoon of thyme,
One tablespoon of finely minced parsley,
One teaspoon of baking powder,
Four tablespoons of water.

Mix to a dough and then work well to blend. Make into small balls the size of a large pea. Drop into the pepper pot and cook for fifteen minutes. Season with salt and pepper and then serve.

FRUIT SOUP

The French, Swiss and Danish housewives serve during the summer a delicious fruit soup. In Normandy, during apple-blossom time, the petals of the fruit are picked as they fall and are used for fruit soup, blossom jelly and perfume and distilled water.

HOW TO MAKE THIS SOUP

You may use any fruit desired; wash to thoroughly cleanse, and to each pint of crushed fruit allow three pints of water. The fruit must be packed solidly. Place in a kettle and cook until the fruit is soft and then rub through a fine sieve. Now measure and add

One-half cup of sugar,
Three tablespoons of cornstarch, dissolved in
Four tablespoons of cold water to each pint

of the fruit puree. Bring to boil and cook five minutes. Remove from the fire and add yolk of one egg. Beat very hard and then fold in stiffly beaten white of egg; season slightly with nutmeg, chill and serve.

Strawberries, blackberries, raspberries, huckleberries, cherries, grapes, currants, apples, peaches, pears, oranges, lemon and quinces may be used for these soups. They are delicious when served ice cold on a hot day.

MEATS

Use oven for baking and boiling and then cook your meats in the old-fashioned English way by direct contact with the flame. This means that you must first place one quart of water and one tablespoon of salt in the broiler pan of the gas range; then place in the roast, steak or chops, upon the broiler; turn every few minutes. The roast must be placed farther from the flame to prevent burning. A good rule for this is to keep roasting meat four inches from the flame, steaks and chops two and one-half inches and fish three inches.

The placing of water in the broiler pan prevents fat from catching fire. This liquid may be allowed to cool and then the fat may be removed and clarified and used for other purposes. Baste roast with one pint of boiling water while cooking.

ROASTING AND BAKING MEATS

Roasting or grilling is done before open fire, the meat being turned frequently, so that all sides may be cooked alike. The meat is basted with its own fat. This method of cooking meat is used daily in Europe, but not much used in this country.

When a piece of meat is large it is roasted. Meat cooked in an oven by radiated heat is frequently called in this country "roasting." It is well known and needs little description. When baking meat always use a wire rack to lift the meat from the bottom of the pan. This will insure even cooking.

Use the broiling oven in the gas range for roasting, placing rack sufficiently low. Have the oven hot enough to brown the meat quickly, then reduce the heat so that it will cook evenly; turn the roast three times during this process.

Allow one-half an hour after placing meat in the oven before counting time. This is necessary so that the meat may reach the required temperature to start cooking.

To bake (oven roast) use same process, using regular oven.

Start counting time after meat is one-half hour in oven and allow twelve minutes to the pound for very rare, fifteen minutes for rare, eighteen minutes for medium and twenty for well done.

Baste the meat with the liquid in the pan every fifteen minutes. Do not add seasoning to the meat while cooking. It is a well-known fact that salt will cause the juices and flavoring of the meat to dissolve and therefore become lost. Season steaks and chops just before serving. Season roasts five minutes before removing from the oven. Always make the gravy after removing the meat from the pan.

NOTE.—Never dish meat on a cold platter. The contact of a cold dish with the hot meat will injure its delicate aroma.

In many portions of France and England chops and steaks are served upon platters set over a bowl of hot water or a special fuel that can be burned in a container that holds the platter. When serving a large steak always have a cover of metal or another hot dish turned over the meat to prevent it chilling.

CORRECT METHOD OF BOILING MEAT

Place the meat in a saucepan of boiling water and then keep the water boiling rapidly for five minutes after the meat is added. Then place the saucepan in a position where it will cook just below the boiling point for the required length of time. Constant and rapid boiling will cause the albumen in the meat to harden; therefore, no amount of cooking afterward will soften the fibre. It will only cause the meat to fall apart without being tender.

It is important to keep the saucepan closely covered. This will prevent the delicate aroma from evaporating.

Braising: Meat is placed in a hot saucepan and turned quickly and frequently. It is cooked in its own juices in a closely covered saucepan.

Steaming: Cooking meat by placing in steam bath or steamer.

Grilling: Cooking meat over a hot fire on a grill made for the purpose.

Broiling: A very hot fire is necessary for this mode of cooking meat. Only the choicest, tenderest, and most delicate cuts are suitable for cooking by this method. The strong heat instantly coagulates the albumen by searing it, thus retaining all its juices and flavor. That this method may be successful it is very necessary that the meat be turned every few minutes. This also insures it being cooked evenly.

Pan Broiling: This is another method of cooking the fine cuts of meat when it is not possible to broil them. Broiled meat is more healthful and also less wasteful than any other form of cooked meat.

TO PAN BROIL

Heat an iron frying pan red hot, then place in it the meat. Turn it constantly.

TIME FOR ROASTING MEAT IN GAS BROILER

Beef, eighteen minutes to the pound.

Lamb and mutton, twenty-one minutes to the pound.

Veal, twenty-five minutes to the pound.

Chicken or duck, eighteen minutes to the pound without filling and twenty-five minutes to the pound with filling.

Fish, fifteen minutes to the pound.

Au gratin dishes, meat pie and various vegetables may be cooked at the same time.

PORK

Pork should be sweet-smelling—the fat clear white and flesh good pinkish color. Loin for chops, crown roast.

BOILED PORK

Plunge pork in boiling water and cook, allowing twenty-five minutes to the pound.

TO ROAST LOIN

Wipe with damp cloth, pat in plenty of flour, place in a roasting pan, place in hot oven for thirty minutes. Now reduce heat to moderate and roast, allowing thirty minutes to the pound; baste with boiling water after meat is in oven one-half hour.

Fresh ham and shoulder may be roasted in same manner.

SPANISH KIDNEY STEW

Cut three pork kidneys in one-inch pieces, rejecting the tubes and fat, and then soak in warm water and one tablespoon of lemon juice for one hour. Drain, and then parboil and drain and blanch under cold water. Now return to saucepan and add just sufficient boiling water to cover. Cook until tender, and then add

One-half cupful of chopped onions,
Two red or green peppers, chopped fine,
One cupful of tomatoes,
One-half cup of cornstarch dissolved in
One-half cup of cold water.

Bring to boiling point and then add

One cupful of cooked beans,
One and one-half teaspoons of salt,
One-half teaspoon of paprika,
One-quarter teaspoon of thyme.

Heat to the boiling point and then serve.

BRAISED SWEETBREADS

Prepare sweetbreads as directed on Page 164 and then remove the tubes and fat and cut into slices. Place two tablespoons of butter in a saucepan and add the sweetbreads and one tablespoon of grated onions, one cup of mushrooms, toss gently until nicely browned and then lift on squares of toast and cover with supreme sauce.

SAUSAGE CAKES

One-quarter pound of pork sausage,
One-half pound of hamburg steak,
Four onions, minced fine,
Three-quarters cup of prepared bread,
Two teaspoonfuls of salt,
One teaspoon of paprika,
Three tablespoons of finely minced parsley.

Mix to thoroughly blend and then form into round sausages. Roll in flour and brown quickly, and then add

One-half cup of boiling water,
One cup of canned tomatoes.

Bring to the boiling point and cook for five minutes. Serve, lift the sausages on fried mush.

To prepare the bread: Soak stale bread in cold water until soft and then press very dry. Measure and then rub through a fine sieve to remove the lumps. All the above may be cooked in the fireless cooker or in casserole dishes.

MUTTON

Mutton is the dressed carcass of the full-grown sheep and is usually prime in animals from three to five years old. If any older than this it lacks flavor and is tough.

The cuts of mutton and of lamb are the same, namely: The meat is divided into fore and hind quarters and then cut into the neck, shoulder, rack, breast, loin and leg.

The shoulder and leg are used for roasting and may be boned and then filled and rolled. For choice rack, cut to the tenth rib as for the chops. Three ribs and the neck for stewing, meat pies, goulashes, etc. The loin for chops.

The French and English have methods of cutting and cooking mutton and lamb that made these cuts delicious.

CHOPS

French chops: Cut two ribs thick from the rack. English chops: Cut two inches thick from the loin, including the kidney.

TO COOK

Trim the chops free from excess fat and then baste with the juice of one lemon. Place in a broiler and cook for ten minutes, turning them frequently.

ENGLISH DRESSING FOR LAMB OR MUTTON CHOPS

One tablespoon of Worcestershire sauce,
Two tablespoons of salad oil,
One teaspoon of mustard,
One-half teaspoon of salt,
One-half teaspoon of paprika,
Juice of one-half lemon.

Blend well together and then spread lightly on both sides of the cooked chops. Serve on a hot platter without gravy, with spiced grape or currant jelly.

ROAST MUTTON

Trim to remove the excess fat and then dust with flour. Place on the rack in the baking pan. Place in a hot oven to brown for thirty minutes. Baste every ten minutes with boiling water. Cook the meat for eighteen minutes to the pound, not counting the first half hour in which the meat starts to cook. Drain off the fat before making the gravy.

Mutton and lamb chops may be used for frying purposes. It can be blended with equal amounts of ham, bacon, pork or beef fat. Save every bit of fat and use it for making soap. This fat makes a fine soft soap for scouring and cleaning.

CURRY OF MUTTON

Have the butcher cut the neck of mutton into cutlets and then wipe with a damp cloth and place in a saucepan, together with

Two medium sized onions,
One carrot, cut in dice.

Gently brown the meat before adding any water. When meat is browned add

Two cups of boiling water.

Cook until tender and then season and thicken the gravy slightly with cornstarch. Now add

One-half teaspoon of curry powder.

To serve, place a border of cooked noodles around the edge of a large platter and then lift the mutton curry in the centre and garnish with finely chopped parsley.

GOULASH

This is a characteristic dish of the Balkan states. It is made by cutting one-half pound of lean beef (shin) into one-inch thick blocks and three-quarters of a pound of veal cut into small pieces. Roll the meat in flour and then place in a stewing pan. Cover with boiling water and cover closely. Cook the meat until it is tender. Remove the lid and boil the liquid quickly to reduce. Now add:

One-half cup of thick sour cream,
One tablespoon of paprika,
Three tablespoons of grated onion,
Two tablespoons of finely minced parsley,
Two teaspoons of salt.

Bring to a boil and then simmer for ten minutes. Serve with fried noodles.

SWEETBREAD PATTIES

To make the patty shells place in a bowl two cups of flour and then add

One teaspoon of salt,
Five teaspoons of baking powder.

Rub between the hands to mix and run into the prepared flour

One-half cup of shortening.

Mix to a dough with a scant two-thirds cup of ice-cold water. Turn on a floured moulding board and either roll or pat out one and one-quarter inch thick. Cut as for biscuits, using a water glass to cut with. The biscuit cutter will not permit cutting with this thickness of dough. Now use small cutter and cut out the centre, leaving about one-half inch thickness at the bottom and a wall one-half inch thick around the patty shell. Place on a baking sheet and bake in a hot oven for eighteen minutes. Then fill with braised sweetbreads.

BRAISED OXTAILS WITH BAKED DRIED PEAS

Soak one and one-half cups of dried peas over night and then in the morning parboil. Place in a baking dish, together with

One-half cup of chopped onions,
Two green peppers, chopped fine,
Two prepared oxtails,
One cupful of tomatoes,
Two teaspoons of salt,
One-half teaspoon of pepper,

and sufficient water to cover. Bake in a moderate oven for three hours.

To prepare the ox-tails have the butcher cut the tails in two-inch pieces and then soak for two hours in lukewarm water. Wash well and parboil for fifteen minutes.

CHILI OF BEEF

Cut one pound of flank steak in one-inch blocks and then roll in flour and brown quickly in hot fat. Now add

Six onions, chopped fine,
Three red pimentoes, chopped fine,
One cup of tomatoes,
One cup of water.

Cook slowly until meat is tender and then season with

Two teaspoons of salt,
One teaspoon of paprika,

and add one cup of cooked beans. Heat to boiling point and then serve.

MEAT LOAF

Two cups of raw meat, minced fine,
One cup of onions, chopped fine,
Two cups of cold cooked oatmeal,

One teaspoon of thyme,
One teaspoon of sweet marjoram,
One tablespoon of salt,
One teaspoon of pepper,
One-half cup of stock to moisten.

Mix thoroughly and then pack into a well-greased and floured loaf-shaped pan. Place this pan in a larger one containing water and bake in a slow oven for one hour. This dish will keep for one week in the icebox. It makes splendid sandwiches.

Select cut from neck then using meat for the loaf

Then cover the bones with cold water and then add

Two onions,
One carrot,
One fagot of soup herbs.

Cook slowly for one hour. Use this liquid for a stock for making gravy.

SWEETBREADS POLASKA

Select medium-sized sweetbreads, place the sweetbreads in cold water to soak, adding one teaspoon of lemon juice; soak for two hours and then wash and pat dry. Remove the tubes and fatty particles and then place in a saucepan. Cover with boiling water and cook for twenty minutes. Blanch under cold running water and let cool. Pat dry and then place in icebox until needed.

Prepare one pint of cream sauce as follows: Place one pint of milk in a saucepan and add six tablespoons of flour. Stir with a wire spoon or fork to dissolve the flour, then place on the stove and bring to a boil. Now add

One level tablespoon of salt.
One level teaspoon of paprika,
Two tablespoons of lemon juice,
One teaspoon of grated rind of lemon,

One-half teaspoon of mustard,
One well-beaten egg.

Beat to thoroughly mix; then add

One cup of cooked peas,
One tablespoon of grated onion,
The prepared sweetbreads, cut into three-quarter inch pieces.

Mix thoroughly and then fill into the patty shells. Sprinkle the top with fine bread crumbs; place and bake in a moderate oven for twenty-five minutes. Now while the patties are heating, peel and wash one-quarter pound of mushrooms, using the stem and button. Parboil and then drain. Pan for four minutes in a little butter and then serve as a garnish with the patties.

CREOLE BEEF

Have the butcher cut two pounds of shin beef, leaving the bone in. Wipe it with a damp cloth and then pat into the meat one-half cupful of flour. Melt five tablespoons of shortening in a deep saucepan, and when hot put in the meat. Brown quickly and then turn on the other side. When both sides are browned add

Two cups of boiling water,
One cup of chopped onions,
Two carrots cut in dice,
One cup of canned tomatoes.

Bring quickly to a boil and cover closely and cook very slowly until tender, usually about two hours. Season and then it is ready to serve; or the pot may be placed in a slow oven for three hours.

SHELL FISH

Shellfish includes crabs, both hard and soft shell, lobsters, shrimp, terrapin, green turtle, snapper, etc.

All shellfish must be actively alive before cooking. This is the essential point and will prevent ptomaine poisoning. Never cook shellfish if they are dead. Remember, they are deadly.

Place a boiler of water on the stove and bring to a boil. Add one tablespoon of red pepper and one cup of vinegar. To cook lobster, shrimp, crabs, etc., cover and cook rapidly for twenty-five minutes for the medium size, fifteen minutes for the small and thirty minutes for the large ones.

When cooked, remove from the water and place under cold water. Let cool. Place on the ice until needed.

To clean crabs break off the claws and then save the two large ones. Then remove the apron pieces of the shell, like a plate under the eyes. Break the shell apart and remove the spongy fingers, sandbag and eggs, if any. Wash well. You now have white oval-shaped pieces of crab meat, that must be picked from its cells. Split with a silver knife and use an oyster fork to pick out the meat. This can be used for au gratin, à la King, ravigotte, deviled crabs, salads, croquettes and crab cakes.

CRAB MEAT

The crab must be actively alive before cooking. To cook place a large boiler of water on the fire and bring to a boil; add to it

One-half cup of vinegar,
One teaspoon of cayenne pepper.

Then add the crabs and cover closely and boil for twenty minutes. Count time when water boils after adding crabs.

FRIED CRAB MEAT

Pick the meat from the cooked crabs and mince fine two ounces of bacon. Place the bacon and one and one-half cups of crab meat and two tablespoons of grated onion in a hot skillet and cook until nicely browned. Serve on toast and pour melted butter over the prepared crab meat.

CRAB MEAT SERVED IN CREAM

Place in a saucepan

One and one-half cups of milk,
Six level tablespoons of flour.

Stir to blend. Bring to a boil and cook for three minutes. Now add

One and one-half cups of crab meat,
One green pepper minced fine,
One onion, grated,
One teaspoon of salt,
One teaspoon of paprika,
Grated rind of one-quarter lemon,
Juice of one lemon,
Two tablespoons of butter.

Toss gently, cooking until well heated. Serve in individual ramekins or small custard cups, dusting with paprika.

FRIED CRABS

Clean the cooked crabs and then cut a thin slice from the shell that contains the meat. Dip the meaty part in a salad oil and fry until golden brown in hot skillet.

RAVIGOTTE SAUCE

One cup mayonnaise,
One-half cup finely chopped young green onions,
One-quarter cup finely chopped parsley,
One-quarter cup finely chopped green peppers,
One-quarter teaspoon mustard,
One teaspoon paprika,
One teaspoon salt.

Beat to mix.

CRAB MEAT BALLS

Mince fine

Two ounces of bacon,
Two green peppers,
One-half cup of canned tomatoes, pressed very dry,
Two tomatoes,
Three onions.

Brown the bacon quickly and then add the finely chopped peppers, tomatoes and onions. Cook gently until soft and dry, then add

One and one-half cups of crab meat,
One teaspoon of salt,
One teaspoon of paprika,
One tablespoon of Worcestershire sauce.

Mix well and then form into balls the size of a fishcake and roll in flour, dip in beaten egg and fry until golden brown in hot fat. Serve with tartare sauce.

CRAB RAVIGOTTE

Serve crab meat in nests of crisp lettuce with ravigotte sauce.

CRAB MEAT A LA KING

Place in saucepan or chafing dish

One and one-half cups of thick cream sauce.

Add

Three-quarters cup of mushrooms, peeled and cut into tiny pieces and parboiled,
Two pimentos chopped fine,
One well-beaten egg,
One teaspoon salt,

One teaspoon paprika,
Juice of one-half lemon,
Two cups or one-half pound of crab meat.

peeled and cut into tiny pieces and parboiled.

Toss with fork to mix; heat to boiling point and serve with toast.

TRIPE AND OYSTERS

Cut one-half pound of cooked tripe into small dice and place in a saucepan and cover with boiling water. Cook for ten minutes and then drain and add

One and one-half cups of thin cream sauce,
One small onion, grated,
Two tablespoons of finely minced parsley,
Twenty-five stewing oysters.

Bring to a boil and cook for eight minutes, then season with

Two teaspoons of salt,
One teaspoon of paprika.

GRILLED OYSTER ON HALF SHELL

Allow four large oysters for each service. Have the oysters opened on the deep shell and remove the oysters, wash free from bits of shell and then roll in grated cheese. Replace on shell and then spread each oyster with one-half teaspoon of minced bacon. Sprinkle with fine bread crumbs and then bake eight minutes in a hot oven or broiler.

OYSTERS ON THE HALF SHELL

Have the oysters opened on the deep shell and remove the oyster. Look over carefully for bits of shell, and then prepare a mixture of

One tablespoon of horse radish, grated,
Three tablespoons of catsup,

One-half teaspoon of salt,
One teaspoon of paprika.

Mix and dip oyster into the sauce, then roll in finely grated cheese. Serve ice cold.

OYSTER COCKTAIL

Sauce for the cocktail can be made from

One-half cup of finely chopped onions.

Place in a saucepan and cook until the onions are soft and then rub through a fine sieve and add

One tablespoon of horseradish,
One tablespoon of Worcestershire sauce,
One teaspoon of salt,
One teaspoon of paprika.

Beat to thoroughly mix and add five small oysters for each service.

OYSTER PIE

Make a pastry of

One cup of flour,
One-half teaspoon of salt,
One teaspoon of baking powder.

Sift and then rub in four tablespoons of shortening, and then mix to a dough with five tablespoons of water. Roll out one-half of the pastry one-quarter inch thick and then line a deep pie tin with the pastry. Then place in layers of the oysters and season with

Salt,
Pepper,
One-quarter teaspoon of grated onion,

One teaspoon of finely minced parsley.

Now another layer of oysters and then the seasoning. Now pour over all one cup of very thick cream sauce. Roll out the balance of the pastry and cut in one-inch-wide strips. Place lattice fashion over the tops of the pie and wash with water and bake in a hot oven for forty-five minutes.

CRAB MEAT AU GRATIN

Place in a bowl

Two cups thick cream sauce,
One and one-quarter cups crab meat,
One onion grated,
Three tablespoons finely minced parsley,
One and one-half teaspoons salt,
One-half teaspoon white pepper,
One-half teaspoon paprika.

Mix with fork, turn into au gratin dish, sprinkle the top with fine bread crumbs, dot with bits of butter and then sprinkle two tablespoons grated cheese and bake in a moderate oven thirty-five minutes.

To prepare cream sauce for à la King and au gratin dishes, use four level tablespoons flour to each cup milk.

Dissolve flour in cold milk, bring to boil, cook two minutes; it is then ready for use.

SOFT SHELL CRABS

Soft-shell crabs are shedders, that is, the crab has shed his shell and the new one is not yet hard. To clean, insert the finger under the apron-shaped piece and the back part of the shell and remove the spongy fingers, the entrails, etc. Wash and drain well and then roll in flour, dip in beaten egg and then roll in fine crumbs and fry until golden brown in hot fat. Place in a hot oven for ten minutes to cook. Serve with tartare sauce.

LOBSTER

Lobster may be boiled, broiled and baked and may be served in same manner as crab meat.

LOBSTER A LA NEWBURG

Place in a saucepan

One and one-half cups of milk,
Five tablespoons of flour.

Dissolve the flour in the milk and bring to a boil. Cook for five minutes and then add

One well-beaten egg,
Lobster meat, cut in one-inch blocks,
One teaspoon of salt,
One teaspoon of paprika,
One-half teaspoon of Worcestershire sauce,
Juice one-half lemon.

TO BROIL LOBSTERS

Split the live lobster in half. Lay it on its back. Do not cut the back shell through. Remove the entrails and remove the vein through the tail. Wash well and then brush with salad oil and place in broiler, shell side up, and cook for fifteen minutes. Turn the flesh side up and baste with salad oil or melted butter. Cook for twelve minutes and then remove and serve with melted butter, chili or tomato sauce.

TO BOIL

Plunge the lobster into boiling water and cook for twenty minutes, for medium lobster. Cool, break apart, discard entrails and fine vein running down the centre of the tail. Break open the claws and remove the meat. This meat and that of the belly and tail may be used for salads, ravigottes, au gratins, croquettes, cutlets, à la King and terrapin style.

SAUCE TO SERVE WITH FISH—FOR BOILED FISH

One cup of fish stock (Court Bouillon),
One-half cup of milk,
Three level tablespoons of cornstarch.

Dissolve the starch in the milk and then add the fish stock. Bring to a boil and cook slowly for eight minutes. Add

One tablespoon of butter,
One teaspoon of salt,
One teaspoon of paprika,
One teaspoon of grated onion,
One well-beaten egg.

Beat thoroughly to mix and then bring to heating point. Serve.

TARTARE SAUCE FOR FRIED FISH

One cup of mayonnaise dressing,
One medium sized pickle, chopped fine,
One tablespoon of grated onion,
Two tablespoons of minced parsley,
One teaspoon of paprika,
One-half teaspoon of mustard,
One teaspoon of salt.

Blend well before serving.

Two tablespoons of butter,
One tablespoon of lemon juice,
One tablespoon of grated onion,
One tablespoon of finely chopped onion,
One teaspoon of salt.

BAKED SHAD

Select a two and one-half pound shad. Have the fish dealer clean and prepare it for baking. Now prepare a filling as follows: Place in a bowl

One cup of breadcrumbs,
Two onions, chopped fine,
Two tablespoons of finely chopped parsley,
One and one-half teaspoons of salt,
One teaspoon of pepper,
One-half teaspoon of thyme,
One egg,
Two tablespoons of salad oil.

Mix well and then fill into the fish. Sew the opening with a stout string and a darning needle. Pat the flour into the fish. Place in a baking pan and bake in a hot oven for one hour. Baste every fifteen minutes with one cup of boiling water. Now, if you place a strip of cheesecloth under the fish you will be able to lift it without breaking. Use the leftover portions for shad au gratin for Monday night's dinner.

PLANKED SHAD

Have the fish dealer split the shad for planking. Soak the plank in cold water for two hours and then place the fish on the plank, and brush it with lemon juice. Place in the lowest part of the broiler of the gas range. Begin to baste with cold water after the fish has been in the oven for twelve minutes. Allow thirty minutes for planking a two and one-half pound shad.

LONG ISLAND DEEP SEA PIE

Grease a deep baking dish and then sprinkle with fine bread crumbs. Now place a layer of finely diced potatoes in the bottom of the dish. Next a layer of cooked fish, cut into pieces the size of a walnut. Next a layer of sliced onions; then a layer of sliced tomatoes; repeat, making two layers. Season each layer with salt, pepper and finely minced parsley. Now prepare a sauce as follows:

Place

One and one-half cups of milk in a saucepan,
Six level tablespoons of flour.

Stir until the flour is dissolved and then bring to a boil. Remove from the fire and add

Two tablespoons of Worcestershire sauce,
One well-beaten egg.

Pour over the prepared pie. Place a crust on top, making three or four gashes in it to permit the steam to escape. Bake in slow oven one hour.

APPETIZERS

The appetizer is a small morsel of food served at the beginning of the meal, causes a free flow of digestive juice and thus helps the digestion. During the growing season these canapés may be scullions, served icy cold, radishes, cold and crisp and cut into thin pieces, but still left on the stem; well-cleaned, crisp, crinkly watercress; coleslaw, with celery; coleslaw with green and red peppers or with scullions, or with bacon or ham nicely browned; or just a slice of full ripe tomato, spread with mayonnaise and dusted with grated cheese or paprika.

Many housewives have the impression that the preparation of the delicious accessories of the cosmopolitan meal is expensive. Well, I hardly need tell you that the French housewife is noted for her thrift and that these dainty tidbits are frequently portions of leftovers from a meal, sometimes the scrapings of a saucepan or a tablespoon of meat, vegetables and gravy.

Have you ever had just a small piece of fish left over, entirely too small to serve by itself? And rather than leave it on a plate or saucer to form an accumulation you think, "Well, I can't use it, so into the garbage it goes."

Now this tablespoon or two of fish would have made you a few delicious canapés; by flaking it and then putting it through a sieve. Place it on a platter and then add

Two tablespoons of butter,
One teaspoon of paprika,
One tablespoon of grated onion,
One tablespoon of finely minced parsley.

Work to a smooth paste and then spread on a narrow strip of toast. Garnish with a slice of hard-boiled egg.

The canapé, though it bears a foreign name, is not necessarily an expensive addition to the menu for the family, nor is it elaborate. This delectable morsel is rather dainty, delicate and used as an appetizer that helps to start and stimulate the digestive juices and thus cause them to flow freely for the digestion of the food.

Canapés are usually served cold, on a plate covered with a doily; the canapé is placed on this. They need not all be alike; the bread may be cut with various sandwich cutters or it may be cut into finger widths and then toasted lightly and spread with the prepared paste.

Meat, chicken, cheese, nuts, olives, etc., may be used in place of the fish. If you have just a spoonful or so of peas, beans, spinach, cauliflower or asparagus you may use it in place of the fish, thus making a vegetable canapé. Try two canned pimentos in place of either meat or fish.

EGG CUTLETS

Make a cream sauce, using six level teaspoons of flour to one cup of milk. Dissolve the flour in the milk and then bring to a boil. Cook for five minutes and then cool and place in a bowl and add two hard-boiled eggs chopped fine and

Two tablespoons of finely chopped parsley,
One tablespoon of finely grated onion,
One and one-half teaspoons of salt,
One teaspoon of paprika,
One-quarter cup of fine bread crumbs.

Mix and then pour on well-greased platter. Cool for four hours. To mould, form into shape and then dip in flour, then in beaten egg and then in fine bread crumbs. Fry until golden brown in hot fat or vegetable oil. Serve with tomato sauce.

BAKED EGGS IN CORN CASES

Make ten corn muffins, from the following mixture:

One and one-quarter cups of milk,
One egg,
Two tablespoons of syrup,
Two tablespoons of shortening.

Beat hard to mix and then add

One and one-quarter cups of sifted flour,
Three-quarters cup of cornmeal,
Five teaspoons of baking powder.

Beat thoroughly to mix and then pour into well-greased muffin pans and bake for thirty-five minutes in a hot oven. Now cut from the top one slice from each of the four muffins and use a spoon to scoop out the centres. Break an egg and then fill to the top with cheese sauce. Sprinkle with bread crumbs and set in a baking pan and bake for twenty minutes in a moderate oven. Serve with either cream or tomato sauce.

SPANISH OMELET

Beat whites of three eggs until stiff, then carefully cut and fold in yolks of three eggs. Then when well blended, pour in hot frying pan containing three tablespoons of shortening; cook slowly, shaking frequently until mixture is dry on top. Now spread with a filling prepared as follows:

Place in a bowl

Two tablespoons grated onion,
One-half cup of well-drained tomatoes,
Four olives, chopped fine,
Two tablespoons of finely minced parsley,
One-half teaspoon of paprika.

Cook this mixture in two tablespoons of shortening until hot, spread on omelet, fold and roll, turn on hot dish, sprinkle with paprika and garnish with finely chopped parsley.

EGGS A LA GRENADIER

Cook three ounces of macaroni and then place in a bowl, and season highly. Add

One onion, chopped fine,
Two tablespoons of finely chopped parsley.

Now fill into five pimentos. Place in a baking pan and bake for fifteen minutes. Remove and then place on a hot platter, flattening well; then place one poached egg on each pepper. Cover with cheese sauce and garnish with parsley.

CODDLED EGGS

Place a teaspoon of butter in an egg glass or custard cup. Break in two eggs, then add one teaspoon of butter and place in a cup of cold water. Bring to a boil and cook for three minutes. Lift cups on saucers, dust the eggs lightly with paprika, and serve. Use two eggs for each service.

How to utilize and serve leftover food so there will be no actual waste has perplexed many young housewives, and as one woman writes me: "I try to keep down the leftovers, but every once in so often they just rise up and conquer me."

Every housewife knows that, no matter how carefully she plans there is sure to be a small quantity of leftover meat, gravy or vegetables. And just what to do with them is almost a daily problem. Two essentials are necessary to successfully utilize leftovers: First, good seasoning; second, attractive appearance.

The French excel in serving leftovers because they so thoroughly understand the art of flavoring and seasoning. The French housewife knows very well that she may only have a *pot au feu* to serve to the family, but the family knows that the delicate, attractive manner in which the food is put on the table would appeal to the epicure, though the table is but a plain ash top, scoured to the whiteness of the snows.

HOW TO PREPARE A FAGGOT OF SOUP HERBS

Place in separate piles:

One branch of parsley,
One-quarter leek,
Two branches of thyme,
One-half carrot, cut lengthwise,
One bay leaf.

Tie in bunches and then dry thoroughly and place in a fruit jar until needed.

FRENCH SEASONINGS

Each housewife prepares her own seasonings from her garden. You know, she grows them in the garden, and as the leaves become abundant she picks them each day, dries them thoroughly, and then places them in separate containers. She prepares the faggots of soup herbs and has them ready for instant use.

GARLIC

Few American persons know of the garlic but as a rank, pungent flavor. To the foreigner garlic is as sweet tasting as the onion and its flavor delightful in food. Just that dash that it needs to give it zest. Separate a clump of garlic into cloves and then peel and place in a fruit jar. Now bring one pint of white wine vinegar to the scalding point and then pour it over the garlic. Place on the cover and set in a warm place for two days. Use this vinegar for seasoning gravies and use the garlic, cut into tiny bits the size of a pinhead, for flavoring.

For serving, use individual ramekin casseroles, baking shells, and thus make for efficient and quick handling of the food, in which the food itself is presented in a most attractive way. A good blend of seasoning is most important, so I am going to give you a French housewife's secret. Mince four medium-sized onions very fine, then place in a bowl and add

Six tablespoons of salt,
Two teaspoons of paprika,
One-half teaspoon of thyme,
One-half teaspoon of sweet marjoram,
One-quarter teaspoon of sage,
Pinch of cloves,
Pinch of allspice.

Rub together until thoroughly mixed and then put in a warm dry place for twenty-four hours. Put through a fine sieve. Place in a bottle and use one teaspoon of this mixture in place of salt.

The average housewife seldom thinks of using such herbs as sweet basil, sorrel, tarragon, leek and chervil, yet they give a delicious flavoring not only to soups, stews, ragouts and goulashes, but to made dishes. They can be grown in the kitchen garden. A good sauce is important, and not only increases the portion, but also gives it an attractive appearance.

Leftover meats and vegetables may be turned into palatable food with just a little time and energy. The basis of all croquettes should be a good thick moulding sauce that will give a product that is creamy and delicious to taste.

Owing to the fact that croquettes and cutlets are usually fried in hot fat, it is not necessary to add either shortening or butter to the cream sauce.

The true secret to good croquettes or cutlets is to have the mixture rich and creamy. Mould into croquettes and then dip in flour and then in the egg mixture and finally roll in fine crumbs. Now fry until golden brown in hot fat.

How to make the foundation:

Place in a saucepan:

One cup of milk,
Seven level tablespoons of flour,

Stir to dissolve the flour and then bring to a boil. Cook slowly for five minutes and then add the flavoring and seasoning. Set aside to cool and then mould. Form into croquettes, roll in flour, dip in beaten egg and then roll in fine bread crumbs and fry until golden brown in hot fat.

NUT AND PEPPER CROQUETTES

Two green peppers,
Two medium-sized onions,

Mince very fine and then parboil and drain. Turn on a cloth and pat dry. Place in a bowl and add

One cup of cream sauce, made as given in the method,
One-half cup of finely chopped nuts,
One teaspoon of salt,
One teaspoon of paprika,
Three tablespoons of grated cheese.

Mix thoroughly and then pour on a large platter and allow to cool, then finish as directed for cheese croquettes.

LIMA BEAN CROQUETTES

Wash and soak overnight three-quarters cup of baby lima beans. In the morning parboil until tender and then drain until very dry. Now put

One green pepper,
Two medium-sized onions,
Four pieces of bacon,

through a food chopper. Place in a pan and cook until the onions and peppers are soft. Drain free from fat and then put the beans through the food chopper and add:

The prepared peppers and onions and bacon,
One teaspoon of paprika,
Two tablespoons of finely minced parsley,
One teaspoon of Worcestershire sauce

Mix thoroughly and then mould into croquettes and dip in flour, then in beaten egg, and roll in fine bread crumbs. Fry until golden brown in hot fat.

Leftover meat may be minced fine and seasoned as follows:

Put a sufficient amount of cold cooked meat or fish through the food chopper to measure three-quarters cup and

One large onion,
Four branches of parsley,

Place the mixture in a bowl and add

One teaspoon of salt,
One teaspoon of paprika,
One cup of cream sauce,

made as directed in the method, then the finely chopped meat and one teaspoon of Worcestershire sauce. Mix thoroughly and then set aside to mould. Form into croquettes and roll in flour, dip in beaten egg and then roll in fine bread crumbs. Fry in hot fat.

Cold beef, lamb, chicken, veal, ham or crab meat or fish may be used for this delectable method of serving an entrée. Nuts, eggs, cheese, both cottage or pot, and store cheese, may be used. Dried peas, lima beans, navy and soy beans as well as cow peas and lentils will afford a splendid variety to the thrifty housewife who must provide cheap protein dishes.

The difference between a croquette and a cutlet is just in the shape. Croquettes are shaped either in the cylindrical or conical forms and cutlets in flat, either round, triangle or chop shape.

To prepare the egg for dipping add four tablespoons of evaporated milk and beat hard to thoroughly blend. Place croquette or cutlet on wire spoon and use tablespoon to pour the beaten egg over the croquette.

To prepare the crumbs dry all pieces of stale bread thoroughly. No bit is too small, a crust or even the crumbs left from cutting the bread. Put the well-dried bread through the food chopper and then sift through the colander; either put the coarse crumbs through the food chopper the second time or keep them for au gratin dishes.

Always serve either cream or tomato sauce with croquettes and cutlets and garnish them with parsley or cress.

BLACKBERRY PUDDING

Place in a mixing bowl:

One cup of flour,
One and one-half cups of fine bread crumbs,
One-half teaspoon of salt,
One tablespoon of baking powder,
One egg,
One and one-half cups of water,
Two cups of well-cleaned blackberries,
One-quarter teaspoon of nutmeg.

Beat to mix and then pour into a pudding dish and bake forty-five minutes in a slow oven. Serve with sweet spiced blackberry sauce.

MARMALADE PUDDING

Place in a mixing bowl:

One and one-half cups of fine bread crumbs,
Three-quarters cup of flour,
One tablespoon of baking powder,
One-half cup of finely chopped suet,
Three-quarters cup of brown sugar,
One teaspoon of nutmeg,
Two eggs,
One cup of milk.

Beat to mix and then grease and flour a mould. Put four tablespoons of marmalade in the bottom and then put in two-inch layer of batter. Spread with the jam and then repeat with the batter. Repeat this process until the mould is three-quarters filled. Have the batter on top. Cover and boil for one hour. Then unmould and serve hot or cold with thin cream.

PEACH CRUMB PUDDING

Grease a baking dish thoroughly and then dust it well with the fine bread crumbs. Now place in a mixing bowl:

Yolk of one egg,
One cup of brown sugar,

Cream and then add

Two tablespoons of shortening,
Two cups of bread crumbs,
Two cups of stewed peaches,
One-half cup of flour,
One tablespoon of baking powder,
One-half teaspoon of nutmeg.

Mix thoroughly and then pour into the prepared baking dish and bake in a slow oven for thirty-five minutes. Let cool and then turn from mould.

COLONIAL CREAM

Wash one-half cup of tapioca through several waters and then place in a saucepan and add one cup of boiling water. Cook until the tapioca is soft and clear. Remove from the fire and partially cool. Pour upon stiffly beaten white of one egg.

Now add

One-half cup of sugar,
One-half cup of cocoanut,
One-half cup of finely chopped nuts.

Beat to thoroughly mix and then pour into sherbet cups. Chill and top with one tablespoon of whipped cream or fruit whip.

RASPBERRY FRUIT BETTY

Cook one box of raspberries with

One-half cup of water,
One-half cup of sugar,

Rub through the sieve to remove the seeds and then measure. Now place one and one-half cups of raspberry puree in a mixing bowl and add

One and one-half cups of fine bread crumbs,
One-half cup of flour,
Two teaspoons of baking powder,
One-half teaspoon of salt,
One-half cup of brown sugar,
One-half teaspoon of cinnamon,
Two tablespoons of melted shortening,
Yolk of one egg.

Beat to mix and then pour into well-greased pudding dish and bake in a moderate oven for thirty minutes. Serve with fruit sauce made from

White of one egg,
One-half glass of jelly.

Beat until this mixture holds its shape. Pour over the fruit whip and a little of the leftover raspberry puree.

RASPBERRY CRUMB PUDDING

Scald two cups of milk and then pour into a bowl and add:

Two tablespoons of shortening,
Three-quarters cup of sugar,
One cup of bread crumbs,
One-half teaspoon of salt.

Beat to mix and then cool and add

One cup of flour,
One egg,
One tablespoon of baking powder,
One and one-half cups of prepared raspberries.

Beat to mix and then pour into a pudding dish and bake for forty minutes in a slow oven. Serve either hot or cold with raspberry fruit sauce.

CHERRY CUSTARD

Stone one-half pound of cherries and then place in a saucepan and add

One cup of sugar,
One-half cup of water.

Cook slowly until the fruit is tender and then measure and place

Two cups of the prepared cherries,
One cup of milk,
Three eggs,

in a bowl and beat to thoroughly mix. Pour into custard cups and then set in a pan of warm water and bake in a moderate oven until firm in the center.

BUTTERMILK BAG PUDDING

Use a pudding cloth to cook this pudding. Wash the cloth in warm water and then rub with shortening and dust with flour. Now place in the mixing bowl

One cup of buttermilk,
Two level teaspoons of baking soda,
One-half cup of sirup,
One cup of brown sugar,
Three-quarters cup of finely chopped suet,
Three cups of flour,
One teaspoon of ginger,
Two teaspoons of cinnamon,
One-half teaspoon of nutmeg,
One cup of seeded raisins, or well-cleansed fresh fruit.

Mix thoroughly, and then tie in the prepared cloth and allow room in it for the pudding to swell. Plunge into boiling water and boil for one and one-quarter hours. Serve with sweetened cream sauce or fruit custard sauce.

VANILLA PUDDING

Three-quarters cup of sugar,
One egg,

Cream well and then add

Four tablespoons of shortening,
One cup of flour,
One cup of bread crumbs,
One teaspoon of salt,
One tablespoon of baking powder,
One cup of milk.

Mix thoroughly and then pour in well-greased mould and boil for one and one-quarter hours or bake for forty-five minutes in a moderate oven. Serve with cream sauce.

BANANA RICE PUDDING

Wash one-quarter cup of rice well and then cook until soft and the water is absorbed in the rice, in one and one-quarter cups of water. Now place in a mixing bowl

Two and one-half cups of milk,
Two eggs,
Three-quarters cup of sugar.

Peel and rub two bananas through a sieve and then beat to mix. Add the rice and then turn into a baking dish and dust with one-half teaspoon of cinnamon. Break into bits one teaspoon of butter and then bake in a slow oven for thirty minutes.

RASPBERRY CUP CUSTARD

Wash and drain one box of raspberries. Place in a saucepan and add

One pint of water,
One cup of sugar.

Bring to a boil and cook until the berries are soft. Rub through a fine sieve. Cool. Now place three eggs in a mixing bowl and add the raspberries and beat the mixture to thoroughly blend. Pour into custard cups and set the cups in a pan containing water. Bake in a slow oven until firm in the centre.

CHOCOLATE CORN STARCH PUDDING

Two cups of milk,
One-half cup of cocoa,
One-fourth cup of cornstarch.

Dissolve the starch in the milk and then bring to a boil and cook slowly for five minutes. Now add

One-half cup of sugar,
One-half teaspoon of vanilla,
One-half teaspoon of cinnamon.

Beat well and then pour into custard cups that have been rinsed in cold water to mould.

OLIVES

OLIVE CANAPE

Use stoned olives for this. Open a bottle of olives, then drain and put through the food chopper, adding

One small onion,
One green pepper,
Three slices of nicely browned bacon,
Four tablespoons of mayonnaise dressing,
One teaspoon of salt,
One teaspoon of paprika.

Mix well and then spread on strips of toast. Garnish with finely chopped white of egg.

OLIVE SALAD

Place in a bowl

One cup of olive meats,
Four slices of nicely browned bacon, cut into tiny bits,
One onion, grated,
Two green peppers, chopped fine,
Three-quarters cup of mayonnaise dressing.

Mix thoroughly and then lift into a nest of crisp lettuce leaves and garnish with slices of hard-boiled egg. This salad is delicious.

OLIVE CHEESE BALLS

Place in bowl

One cup of cottage or pot cheese,
One red pepper, minced very fine,
One tablespoon of grated onion,
One-half cup of finely chopped olives,
One teaspoon of salt,
One-half teaspoon of paprika.

Form into balls and then place in a nest of lettuce. Serve with French dressing.

MACARONI, OLIVES AND CHEESE

This dish is famous among the mountain folk in Italy and it is served on gala days. Cook four ounces of macaroni for fifteen minutes in boiling water and then drain and blanch under cold water. Cool, chop fine, and now add

One-half cup of pimento olives, chopped fine,
One-half cup of grated cheese,
Two cups of cream sauce,
One large onion, minced fine,
Two large red peppers, minced fine,
Two teaspoons of salt,
One teaspoon of paprika,

and a tiny piece of garlic. Mix and then pour into baking dish. Dot the top with bits of butter. Place in a hot oven for twenty-five minutes.

OLIVE FILLING FOR MEAT AND POULTRY

Two and one-half cups of prepared bread crumbs,

One-half cup of finely chopped onions,
One-quarter cup of finely chopped parsley,
One-half cup of finely chopped olives,
One and one-half teaspoons of salt,
One-half teaspoon of paprika,
One-quarter teaspoon of sweet marjoram,
One egg,
Four tablespoons shortening.

Mix thoroughly and then use for filling meat and poultry. This filling is delicious.

To prepare the bread, soak stale bread in cold water until soft and then place in a cloth and press dry. Rub through a sieve and then measure. Use one-half cup of finely chopped stuffed olives to one cup of mayonnaise dressing.

OLIVE SANDWICH FILLING

Put through the food chopper:

One bottle of stuffed olives,
Two red peppers,
One onion,
Four branches of parsley,

Place in a bowl and add

One-half cup of mayonnaise dressing,
One teaspoon of salt,
One-half teaspoon of paprika.

Mix well and then spread between the thinly sliced bread.

OLIVE SANDWICHES

Remove the stones from one large bottle of queen olives and add

One onion,
Two red peppers,

Put through the food chopper and then add

Three-quarters cup of mayonnaise,
One teaspoon of salt,
One and one-half teaspoons of paprika.

Mix and then spread on the prepared bread.

OLIVE SAUCE

Mince fine, using the food chopper, a sufficient amount of olives, after removing the stones, to measure one-half cup. Place in a saucepan and add

One and one-half cups of cream sauce,
Two tablespoons of salt,
One-half teaspoon of paprika,
One-quarter teaspoon of mustard.

Blend well and then bring to the boiling point and serve. This sauce may be made, for variety's sake, with one and one-half cups of tomato sauce to replace the cream sauce; then add two tablespoons of grated cheese. Heat and serve.

SPANISH MEAT LOAF

Place in a bowl

One and one-half cups of prepared bread,
One cup of finely minced cold-cooked mutton,
One cup of pimento olives, chopped fine,
One-half cup of finely minced onions,
One egg,
Two teaspoons of salt,
One teaspoon of paprika,
One-quarter teaspoon of thyme,

One-half cup thick cream sauce.

Mix thoroughly and then pack into the prepared loaf-shaped pan. Place in a larger pan containing hot water and then bake in a moderate oven for forty minutes. Serve with olive sauce. To prepare bread, soak stale bread in cold water; press dry; rub through fine sieve.

OLIVE AND CLAM COCKTAIL

Use olive meats for this. Olive meats are pieces of olives cut from large olives and packed in jars. There are no stones nor waste. Place in a small bowl

Three tablespoons of chili sauce,
One tablespoon of horseradish,
One tablespoon of lemon juice,
One-quarter cup of olive meats,
One teaspoon of salt,
One teaspoon of paprika,
One tablespoon of grated onion.

Mix thoroughly and then divide into four cocktail glasses. Add three cherrystone or little-neck clams to each glass.